Lundy Cookery

Recipes for a small island

by

Ilene Sterns

• CORYDORA PRESS •

Published in Great Britain by

Corydora Press
Ampney Crucis
Cirencester
Gloucestershire GL7 5RY

www.corydora.co.uk

ISBN 978-0-9566532-1-5

This book is printed on recycled paper manufactured from 100% post-consumer waste.

CONTENTS

INTRODUCTION

Whether you are visiting Lundy for the day or staying for a fortnight, the island's shop will be one of your first stops. At first glance, the shop looks like a typical village store: souvenirs, ice lollies and cold drinks jostle for space with sacks of potatoes, frozen foods and jars of jam. But Lundy is no ordinary island and its shop is no ordinary shop – in fact, it is a superstore in miniature.

In Lundy's remote location, who would expect to find coconut milk, pesto or capers? But the shop has them all, along with two kinds of peanut butter, hot pepper sauce and chutney. Naan bread, pitta and baguettes join wholemeal loaves in a veritable United Nations of bread. Further exploration reveals Lundy lamb, tuna steaks, hummus and tempting cheeses, along with a wide range of seasonal fruits and vegetables. But even a superstore can't stock everything. So if you are hoping to find fresh herbs, bagels or passata, you will be disappointed (unless, of course, you've ordered those items in advance).

With so much choice, self-catering visitors will leave the shop filled with inspiration. How about a light lunch of creamy broccoli and blue cheese soup, then homemade scones for tea? But wait – you'll need a liquidiser to puree the soup and scales to weigh the flour for the scones. And unfortunately, you won't find either of those items in a Lundy self-catering kitchen. Nor will you find other basics such as toasters or loaf tins. So you'll have to be creative if you want to prepare interesting meals on Lundy, and that's where this book comes in.

I wrote *Lundy Cookery* to combine my love of good food with my love of Lundy. Having lived and travelled in many countries, I wanted to bring a taste of world cuisine to my favourite island. So I've included recipes from nations as diverse as Italy, China, Morocco and the US. Yet all the dishes can be made using ingredients that are regularly available in the island's shop.

Most of the book's recipes are simple and quick to prepare, so you won't be stuck in the kitchen when you'd rather be outdoors. And I have specified quantities as volumes rather than weights, so you will be able to create any dish (even baked goods) using the standard Lundy kitchen equipment.

Lundy Cookery also includes a special chapter called 'Salmagundi', which is all about minimising food waste. If, for example, you've got a bit of mayonnaise left in the fridge, turn to Salmagundi's alphabetical list of ingredients. There you will find links to recipes that use mayonnaise, along with ideas for turning small amounts of it into quick and tasty dishes.

I hope you will be inspired by *Lundy Cookery* – not just during your stay on the island, but also after your return to the mainland. If you have comments or suggestions, I'd love to hear them. I can be contacted via Corydora Press (www.corydora.co.uk).

PREFACE TO THE SECOND EDITION

When the first edition of *Lundy Cookery* was published in early 2010, I never could have guessed that two printings would sell out within 18 months. But that's exactly what's happened. The book has also proved popular in its electronic format, which is ideal for anyone who likes to travel light (a necessity for Winter visitors to the island!).

Rather than go for a third printing, I've decided to take this opportunity to create a new edition of *Lundy Cookery*. I've added more recipes as well as additional tips to help you to make the most of your self-catering holiday on the island. Based on requests from readers, I've created some recipes for fresh mackerel and have added some lamb dishes (Lundy lamb is second to none and it's always available in the shop). I've also expanded the 'Salmagundi' section to cover more ingredients. In fact, eagle-eyed readers will discover new recipes and tips throughout the book.

I'd like to take this opportunity to thank everyone who bought the first edition of *Lundy Cookery* – your support and encouragement have been a real inspiration to me. I hope you will enjoy this second edition of the book as much as you did the first.

ACKNOWLEDGEMENTS

The impetus for *Lundy Cookery* comes from Phil Atkin, who suggested (on a very cold and windy December night in Castle Keep East) that I should follow my dream to write a cookery book. So to Phil, my sincere thanks and also all my love. I owe you a huge debt of gratitude.

I would also like to thank Nigel Dalby, Patrizia Fursdon and Fiona McKenzie for their time, encouragement and expertise. This book would not have been possible without them.

QUANTITIES AND MEASUREMENTS

T he recipes in this book have been created specifically for the self-catering visitor to Lundy Island. Because the properties do not have scales, ingredients have to be measured by volume rather than weight. Although it might seem strange to pour 250ml of flour into a measuring jug, anyone who is used to cooking from American recipe books will be familiar with the process. However, in the US, cooks use cup measures, rather than our millilitres.

Lundy Cookery specifies many of its ingredients in millilitres, so the Pyrex measuring jug found in every property should be used to measure everything – even dry ingredients such as flour or sugar. To ensure accurate quantities (particularly when baking) pour or spoon dry ingredients into the jug and then level their tops.

Although volumes are used throughout *Lundy Cookery*, you will find a few ingredients specified by weight. Those items tend to be foods that are sold in tins or pre-packed by weight. For example, a recipe may call for a 400g tin of tomatoes or 100g of butter. In those instances, you can easily estimate the correct quantity based on the amount in the tin or packet.

With the exception of the Baking chapter, most of the recipes in this book are quite flexible. If a stew calls for three carrots and you only have two, don't rush out to buy a third. The dish will be fine without it. Baked goods, on the other hand, do demand a certain amount of precision. Unless you are an experienced baker, it's best to stick to the recipe as written.

As for number of servings: most of the recipes in *Lundy Cookery* have been designed to serve either 2 or 4 people. But they can all be doubled, except for baked goods (which again, are a law unto themselves). Just be aware that if you are increasing quantities from 4 servings to 8, the dish may take longer to cook, or you may have to split the dish into two pans so that it cooks evenly.

******

SOUPS

Mediterranean Fish Soup
(Serves 2, recipe can be doubled)

Based on a traditional Bouillabaisse, this soup is made with frozen seafood for a quick and tasty meal. It is best when served with Mock Rouille (page 95), which enriches the dish and livens up the flavours. You can use frozen cooked prawns in Mediterranean Fish Soup, but if you do, defrost them in advance and add them at the very last minute, heating just long enough to warm them through.

1 small onion, finely chopped

1 large clove garlic, finely minced

2 tablespoons olive oil

3 sticks celery, chopped into 2cm lengths

1 medium potato, chopped into 1cm cubes

400g tin chopped tomatoes

400ml water

1 chicken stock cube, crumbled

½ teaspoon dried thyme

1 bay leaf

1 strip orange peel

A few drops of hot pepper sauce

250g uncooked prawns or white fish such as cod or halibut (no need to defrost if frozen)

Heat the olive oil in a large heavy pot. Add the onion, garlic and a large pinch of salt and cook until soft, about 5 minutes. Add all the other ingredients except the prawns or fish and bring to the boil. Cover the pot and simmer over low heat for 10 minutes.

Add the seafood to the soup and simmer gently for another 8-10 minutes, or until it is cooked through. If you are using fish, break it into large chunks with a spoon as it cooks. Remove the orange peel and bay leaf before serving. Serve immediately in heated bowls, with crusty bread. Stir a spoonful of Mock Rouille (page 95) into each bowl before eating.

****

Irish Lamb Soup
(Serves 4)

Loosely based on the traditional Irish stew, this hearty soup keeps well and tastes even better the next day. You can vary the vegetables according to season or availability: swede, turnip, cabbage or parsnip can be substituted for any of the vegetables in the recipe.

1 tablespoon vegetable oil

700g boneless Lundy lamb, defrosted, cut into small cubes

1 large onion, chopped

2 leeks, rinsed well and sliced

1 litre water

2 beef stock cubes, crumbled

1 teaspoon dried thyme

2 large potatoes, cut into small cubes

2 carrots, sliced

Salt and ground black pepper, to taste

Heat the oil in a large pan and brown the lamb in batches, turning so that it is well browned on all sides. Remove the lamb from the pan and reserve. Add the onions to the pan and cook for 4-5 minutes, until the onions are golden brown. Return the meat to the pan and add the leeks. Pour in the water, add the stock cubes and thyme and bring to the boil. Reduce the heat, cover, and simmer gently for 1 hour.

Add the potatoes and carrots and simmer for an additional 40 minutes, or until the lamb is tender. Remove the pan from the heat and leave it to stand for 5 minutes, then skim the fat off the surface. Add salt and pepper to taste and serve immediately in warmed bowls, or cool and chill. To serve, reheat gently (do not boil).

****

Fish Chowder
(Serves 4-6)

A New England classic, this simple, creamy soup can be made with almost any white fish or shellfish. Clam chowder is traditional, as is cod, but prawn, scallop and even lobster chowder can be found on menus in the fishing ports of Maine and Massachusetts. If you are using frozen fish in your Fish Chowder, defrost it before cooking.

1 litre milk

150ml double cream

700g cod fillets (or other fish or seafood), skin removed

50g butter

1 large onion, chopped

3 medium potatoes, peeled and chopped into cubes

Salt and ground black pepper, to taste

Put the milk and cream into a large pan and bring to the boil. Add the fish and return the liquid to the boil. Reduce the heat and simmer for 2-3 minutes, then remove the pan from the heat and let stand for about 5 minutes, until the fish is just cooked. Remove the fish from the pan and using a fork, flake it into large chunks. Cover the fish and reserve.

Heat the butter in a large pan and add the onion and a large pinch of salt. Cook, stirring occasionally, over medium heat for 5 minutes. Add the potatoes and the milk

mixture used for cooking the fish and bring to the boil.
Reduce the heat, cover the pan and simmer gently for 15
minutes or until the potatoes are tender. Return the fish
chunks to the soup and heat gently for 1-2 minutes. Season
with salt and plenty of black pepper. Serve in warmed
bowls.

****

Soupe au Pistou
(Serves 4)

A traditional recipe from Provence, this simple soup shows off the flavours of fresh summer vegetables. An extra burst of flavour comes from the last-minute addition of a pesto-like basil sauce called pistou (ready-made pesto makes a fine substitute). If you can't find the vegetables below, feel free to use whatever looks freshest. Soupe au Pistou is suitable for vegetarians and it makes a lovely summer supper served with crusty bread and cheese.

2 tablespoons olive oil

1 large onion, chopped

1 courgette, chopped into small cubes

2 tomatoes, seeded and chopped

A handful of green beans, chopped into 2cm lengths

2 carrots, chopped into small chunks

1 celery stick, chopped

1 medium potato, chopped into small cubes

2x400g tins beans (red kidney, chick peas or whatever takes your fancy), drained

2 litres water

4 vegetable stock cubes, crumbled

Salt and ground black pepper, to taste

Ready-made pesto, to serve

Heat the oil in a large saucepan, add the onion and a large pinch of salt and cook over low heat until the onion is soft. Add the courgette, tomatoes, green beans, carrots, celery and potato and stir over medium heat for 3-4 minutes, until the vegetables start to soften.

Add the beans, water and stock cubes and stir well to dissolve the cubes. Bring the soup to the boil, reduce the heat, cover and simmer until all the vegetables are soft, about 30 minutes. Add salt and pepper to taste. Serve in heated bowls, passing the pesto separately so each person can stir a spoonful into his or her bowl before eating.

****

Potato, Leek and Bacon Soup
(Serves 4)

A hearty, warming soup, ideal after a cold morning's walk. Smoked bacon is especially good in this recipe, but if you've only got unsmoked, go ahead and use it – the soup will be just as nice. Potato, Leek and Bacon Soup is best made in advance, as it needs time for the flavours to blend.

1 tablespoon olive oil

125g bacon, cut into small bits

5 medium leeks (white part only), rinsed well and sliced

4 medium potatoes, peeled and cubed

1 litre cold water

3 chicken stock cubes, crumbled

Salt and ground black pepper, to taste

In a large pot, heat the olive oil over medium-high heat. Add the bacon, reduce the heat and brown thoroughly. Pour off any excess fat. Add the leeks and potatoes and stir well. Cover and cook over low heat, stirring occasionally, until the leeks have softened (10-15 minutes).

Add the water and stock cubes and stir well. Bring to the boil, reduce the heat and simmer, covered, for 45 minutes. Season to taste. Cool, cover and chill for at least 1 hour (and ideally overnight). To serve, reheat gently (do not boil) and serve in warmed bowls with plenty of ground black pepper.

SALADS

Middle Eastern Cauliflower Salad
(Serves 4)

Middle Eastern Cauliflower Salad is a light dish with a rich flavour, and it is very moreish! Try it as part of a mixed salad plate or serve it with Mediterranean-style grilled lamb (page 97).

1 cauliflower, divided into florets

2 tablespoons olive oil

Salt and pepper, to taste

100ml natural yoghurt

2 tablespoons peanut butter

Juice of 1 lemon

1 tablespoon mint sauce

Heat the oven to 200 degrees C. Place the cauliflower florets in a roasting tin along with the olive oil, salt and pepper, and give everything a good stir to mix. Roast for 45 minutes or until the cauliflower is browned and tender. Remove from the oven and allow to cool.

For the dressing: mix the yoghurt, peanut butter, lemon juice and mint sauce in a large bowl. Add the cauliflower and mix well. Season to taste and chill until ready to serve. This salad tastes even better after a day in the fridge.

Greek Pasta Salad
(Serves 4)

This vegetarian salad will please everyone, and it is perfect for a summer picnic. Don't be put off by the long list of ingredients; Greek Pasta Salad is simple to make and it can sit in the fridge for several hours (or even overnight) without losing its freshness.

250g pasta shells (or another small shape), cooked, drained and rinsed under cold water until cool then drained again

50ml olive oil

1 medium aubergine, cut into 2cm cubes

½ teaspoon salt

2 garlic cloves, finely minced

Juice of one lemon

2 tablespoons water

1 green pepper, chopped

1 cucumber, seeded and chopped

2 tomatoes, chopped

1 celery stick, sliced

2 spring onions, sliced

1 teaspoon dried oregano

Salt and black pepper to taste

100g feta cheese, crumbled

12 olives, stoned and cut in half

Heat the olive oil in a large pan and add the aubergine. Cover and cook for 3 minutes on medium heat. Stir in the salt, garlic, lemon juice and water; cover and simmer for 6-8 minutes, or until the aubergine is almost tender. Add the green pepper and the dried oregano and simmer for a few more minutes until the peppers have softened.

While the vegetables are cooking, place the cucumbers, tomatoes, celery and salad onions in a large bowl. Add the cooked vegetables, then stir in the cooked pasta and mix well. Add salt and pepper to taste, along with some additional olive oil and lemon juice if the salad seems dry. Refrigerate until about an hour before you are ready to serve. Serve the salad at room temperature, topped with the crumbled feta cheese and halved olives.

****

Apple and Blue Cheese Salad
(Serves 2, recipe can be doubled)

This salad is perfect for winter meals, when fresh vegetables are in short supply. It is crunchy and full of flavour, so it makes a refreshing starter for a hearty main course.

1 apple, cored and cut into 1.5cm cubes

2 celery stalks, thinly sliced

100g blue cheese, crumbled

Handful of mixed nuts, coarsely chopped (optional)

Salad leaves, to serve 2

1 tablespoon vinegar or lemon juice

1 tablespoon olive oil

1 teaspoon runny honey

Salt and ground black pepper, to taste

Combine the apples, celery, blue cheese and nuts (if using) in a serving bowl. Rinse and dry the salad leaves, tear them into bite-sized pieces and add them to the bowl. For the dressing, whisk together the vinegar (or lemon juice), olive oil and honey. Add salt and pepper to taste. Pour the dressing over the salad, mix well and serve immediately.

Chinese-style Cabbage Salad
(Serves 4)

A light, Chinese-influenced 'cole slaw' which is lovely for picnics but also makes a refreshing winter salad. Start making Chinese-style cabbage salad a couple of hours before you plan to eat it, as the vegetables need time to absorb the dressing.

½ green cabbage, cored and very thinly shredded

2 carrots, grated

½ red pepper, cored, seeded and cut into fine slivers

4 spring onions, finely chopped

120ml vinegar

60ml sugar

60ml vegetable oil

1 tablespoon grated fresh ginger

Salt, to taste

50g roasted peanuts, finely chopped

In a serving bowl, combine the cabbage, carrots, red pepper and spring onions. In another bowl, mix together the vinegar, sugar, oil, ginger and salt.

At least one hour before serving, pour the dressing over the vegetables and mix well. Sprinkle the peanuts over the salad just before serving.

Beetroot and Orange Salad
(Serves 4)

The ingredients for this salad are available year round, so it is a useful dish to have in your repertoire.

4 large cooked beetroot, sliced

80ml walnuts or mixed nuts, chopped

2 large oranges

2 tablespoons vinegar

2 tablespoons orange juice

Zest of ½ orange, grated or finely minced

60ml olive oil

Salt and ground black pepper, to taste

Salad leaves for 4 people

Cut the peel off the oranges, trim their tops and bottoms and cut the oranges into thin rounds. Make a vinaigrette dressing with the vinegar, orange juice, zest and olive oil. Add salt and pepper to taste.

Mix the sliced beetroot with half of the vinaigrette. Arrange the salad leaves on a serving dish and top with the beetroot and the orange slices. Drizzle over the remaining vinaigrette and sprinkle with the chopped nuts. Serve immediately.

Marinated Cucumbers
(Serves 6)

This simple salad needs to be made in advance, but once made it will keep for a couple of days. Make Marinated Cucumbers for a summer picnic, or serve them at any time of year as part of a crudités platter.

2 large cucumbers, peeled and very thinly sliced
1 tablespoon salt
150ml vinegar
120ml sugar

Mix the cucumbers with salt in a large bowl. Cover and refrigerate for 45 minutes. Rinse the cucumbers and drain them well.

In the same large bowl, stir together the vinegar and sugar until the sugar has dissolved. Add the cucumbers and mix thoroughly. Cover the salad and chill it for at least 1 hour before serving.

LAMB, PORK AND BEEF

Soutzsoukakia (Greek Meatballs)
(Serves 4)

These sausage-shaped meatballs hail from Smyrna (in Asia Minor), which was home to a large Greek community. The dish is a rich and hearty one, ideal for a cold evening. Serve Soutzsoukakia over boiled rice or couscous for a delicious meal.

Meatballs

450g Lundy lamb mince, defrosted

1 medium onion, finely chopped

2 cloves garlic, finely chopped

2 slices bread, torn into very small bits

75ml red wine

1 teaspoon dried oregano

1 tablespoon mint sauce (if you have it)

1 teaspoon cinnamon

1 egg

1 teaspoon salt

Pepper to taste

Oil for shallow frying

Sauce

2 cloves garlic, finely chopped

400g tin chopped tomatoes

100ml red wine

½ teaspoon cinnamon

Salt and pepper, to taste

First, make the sauce: combine all the sauce ingredients in a small saucepan and bring to the boil. Turn the heat down, cover and simmer gently whilst making the meatballs.

To make the meatballs: combine all the meatball ingredients (except the oil for frying) and mix well. Wet your hands (so the mixture doesn't stick to them) and roll the meat mixture into small sausage-shaped rolls, about 5cm long. Heat the oil in a frying pan and fry the meatballs over medium heat, turning until they are evenly browned and cooked through. (You will need to do this in batches, so that the meatballs brown up nicely – if they are too crowded, they will steam instead of browning.)

As each batch of meatballs is done, remove them to a plate and drain off any excess oil. When the meatballs are all cooked, return them to the frying pan and pour over the tomato sauce. Heat until the meatballs are warmed through and serve over rice or couscous.

****

Moroccan Lamb Stew
(Serves 2, recipe can be doubled)

Moroccan cuisine often combines meat with dried fruits. In this recipe, lemon juice balances the sweetness of the fruit, and the fragrant sauce is enhanced by cinnamon and ginger. Like all stews, Moroccan Lamb Stew can be made ahead of time – it will taste even better the next day. Serve with boiled rice to soak up all the lovely sauce.

450g boneless Lundy lamb, defrosted, cut into big chunks

1 tablespoon olive oil

1 red onion, chopped

2 cloves garlic, finely chopped

4 large carrots, cut into chunks

½ teaspoon ground cinnamon

1 tablespoon fresh ginger, finely chopped or grated

Juice of 1 lemon

100g dried fruit: apricots, prunes or sultanas

2 teaspoons soy sauce

1 teaspoon honey

Water

Salt and pepper to taste

Heat the olive oil in a large pan. Season the lamb with salt and pepper and brown it on all sides in the oil. Remove the browned lamb and reserve. Add the onion, garlic and a large pinch of salt to the oil and cook until soft, about 5 minutes. Return the lamb to the pan, add the carrots, cinnamon and ginger and cook over low heat, stirring constantly, for 1-2 minutes.

Turn up the heat under the pan, add enough water to come part-way up the lamb, add the lemon juice, honey, dried fruit and soy sauce, mix well and bring to the boil. Reduce the heat, cover and simmer gently over very low heat for about 1 hour, or until the meat is tender. Serve with boiled rice.

****

Indian-style Lamb with Aubergine
(Serves 4)

A tomato-based curry sauce brings an Asian flavour to Lundy lamb. This versatile sauce makes an equally good vegetarian main; simply substitute cauliflower, cabbage or leeks for the lamb and braise until tender. Indian-Style Lamb can be made a day ahead as it reheats beautifully and tastes even better the next day. Serve with boiled rice and pass a dish of cooling Cucumber Raita (page 94).

3 tablespoons vegetable or olive oil

700g boneless Lundy lamb, defrosted, cut into 2.5cm cubes

1 medium onion, chopped

2 garlic cloves, finely minced

1 tablespoon grated fresh ginger

1 teaspoon curry powder

Hot pepper sauce, to taste (optional)

2x400g tin chopped tomatoes

1 teaspoon sugar

1 medium aubergine, cut into 2.5cm cubes

400g tin chick peas, drained

Salt and ground black pepper, to taste

Heat 2 tablespoons of the oil in a heavy large casserole or pan over high heat. Working in batches, brown the lamb on all sides. Remove the meat from the pan, season it generously with salt and pepper and reserve.

Add the remaining tablespoon of oil to the pan and reduce the heat to medium. Add the onion, garlic, ginger, curry powder and hot pepper sauce (if using) and cook, stirring constantly, for 2 minutes. Add the tomatoes and the sugar, increase the heat to medium-high and cook until the mixture thickens, stirring constantly (about 6 minutes).

Return the lamb and any juices to the pan and stir to coat the meat with the sauce. Cover and simmer for 1 hour. Add the aubergine and stir to coat it with the sauce. Cover and simmer for an additional 15 minutes. Stir in the chick peas, then cover and simmer for 10 minutes longer. Uncover the pan and cook the stew for a final 5 minutes, in order to thicken the sauce. Season to taste and either cover and chill overnight, or serve immediately on warmed plates.

****

Lamb with Lentils and Rosemary
(Serves 4)

This sophisticated dish is elegant enough to serve to guests, but easy enough for a family supper. If you don't have time to cook the lentils, feel free to substitute tinned cooked beans – the dish will be just as nice.

250ml dried lentils

500ml water

1 chicken stock cube

1 teaspoon dried rosemary, crumbled

1 clove garlic, very finely chopped

1 tablespoon vinegar

A pinch of sugar

Salt and ground black pepper, to taste

3 tablespoons olive oil

100g leaf spinach, shredded

150g feta cheese, crumbled

4 Lundy lamb chops or cutlets, defrosted

Rinse the lentils and drain well. In a medium pan, bring the water to the boil and crumble in the stock cube. Add the lentils and rosemary, reduce the heat and simmer for 20-25 minutes or until tender. Drain the lentils and set aside in a large bowl to cool slightly. (If you are using tinned beans, drain them, add the rosemary and warm gently in a saucepan before proceeding with the next step.)

To make the dressing: mix the garlic, vinegar, sugar and salt/pepper to taste in a small bowl. Whisk in the 3 tablespoons olive oil, stirring till the mixture is smooth and thick. Add the spinach and feta cheese to the lentils, pour over the dressing and mix well. Add pepper to taste (do not add salt as the feta is already quite salty).

Season the lamb. Grill until cooked to your liking and remove from the heat. Whilst the lamb is cooking, divide the lentil mixture into four portions and arrange on warmed plates. Top with the grilled lamb and serve immediately.

****

Lamb and Bean Hotpot
(Serves 2, recipe can be doubled)

Most stews require long slow cooking, but this hotpot is ready to eat in only half an hour. For an easy, warming winter supper, serve Lamb and Bean Hotpot with a mound of creamy mashed potatoes and some steamed broccoli or green beans.

350g Lundy lamb, defrosted and cubed

1 tablespoon olive oil

1 medium onion, finely chopped

1 clove garlic, finely minced

400g tin chopped tomatoes

400g tin butter beans, drained

1 teaspoon dried rosemary, crumbled

Salt and ground black pepper, to taste

Heat the olive oil in a large pan. Brown the lamb cubes on all sides; remove and reserve. Add the onion, garlic and a pinch of salt to the hot oil and cook, stirring, until the vegetables soften. Return the meat to the pan and add the tomatoes, butter beans and rosemary. Cover and simmer gently for 20 minutes. When the lamb is tender, season the stew to taste and serve on warmed plates.

Orange-glazed Pork Chops
(Serves 6)

A sweet and sour orange sauce turns pork chops or steaks into a special treat. Orange-glazed Pork Chops are especially nice when served with boiled rice, but mashed sweet potatoes also make a good accompaniment.

6 pork chops or steaks, defrosted
1 tablespoon olive oil
175ml orange juice
3 tablespoons soft brown sugar
3 tablespoons orange marmalade
1 ½ tablespoons vinegar
Salt and ground black pepper, to taste

Season the pork with salt and pepper. Heat the olive oil in a frying pan and brown the meat on both sides. Do not crowd the pan; brown the pork in two batches if necessary.

Drain off the excess fat. Combine the orange juice, brown sugar, marmalade and vinegar in a jug and stir well to blend. Pour the mixture over the pork in the frying pan and bring to the boil over medium heat. Reduce heat, cover and simmer gently for about 45 minutes, or until the meat is tender. Serve the pork with the sauce spooned over.

Pork with Apples and Ginger
(Serves 4)

Pork has a natural affinity for fruit, as this elegant recipe demonstrates. If you haven't got any apples, pears make a fine substitute. Serve with boiled rice and a simple green vegetable.

4 pork chops or steaks, defrosted
2 tablespoons olive oil
Plain flour (to coat meat)
2 apples, peeled, cored and thinly sliced
75ml dry white wine
2 tablespoons sugar
2 tablespoons crystallised ginger, chopped
Salt and ground black pepper, to taste

Season the pork with salt and black pepper, then coat it on all sides in the flour (shake off excess). Heat the olive oil in a large frying pan over medium heat. Add the pork and brown on both sides, about 3 minutes per side. Remove the pork from the pan and reserve.

Drain excess fat from pan. Add the apples and cook over medium heat for 2 minutes. Stir in the wine, sugar and ginger, scraping up any browned bits. Increase heat to high and boil until the apples are tender and syrup is thick, about 5 minutes. Return the pork to the pan and simmer gently until just cooked through, about 2 minutes. Season to taste.

Blue Cheese Burgers
(Serves 4)

A sophisticated version of the ever-popular burger. For a casual meal, the classic combination of burgers and chips is hard to beat. But for something a bit more elegant, try Blue Cheese Burgers served on warmed plates accompanied by Hasselback Potatoes (page 89) and a steamed green vegetable.

450g beef mince, defrosted

1 tablespoon Dijon mustard

2 spring onions, finely chopped

1 clove garlic, finely chopped

Salt and pepper, to taste

85g blue cheese, crumbled

Preheat the grill. Place the beef, Dijon mustard, spring onions, garlic and seasonings into a large bowl and mix well. Form the beef mixture into four burgers and place the burgers on the grill pan. Grill for 3 minutes.

Turn the burgers over and grill for another 3 minutes (for medium rare) or longer, until cooked to desired doneness. Divide the blue cheese into four equal portions and top the burgers with the cheese. Grill for 1 minute longer, just until cheese is bubbling. Serve immediately.

Beef Braised in Ale
(Serves 4)

Loosely based on the Belgian classic, Carbonnade de Boeuf, this stew develops a deep rich flavour as it simmers away in a slow oven. Once you've put Beef Braised in Ale on to cook, it doesn't need any attention, so it is ideal for a dinner with friends. And like all stews, it tastes even better the next day. Serve with creamy mashed potatoes and perhaps some horseradish sauce, for anyone who would like to add a bit of a kick.

2 tablespoons olive oil

700g stewing beef, defrosted and cubed

2 large onions, chopped

1 tablespoon soft brown sugar

1 tablespoon plain flour

2 tablespoons balsamic (or other) vinegar

500ml strong ale

Salt and ground black pepper, to taste

Preheat the oven to 150 degrees C. Heat 1 tablespoon of the olive oil in a large ovenproof casserole or pan with a lid. Brown the beef on all sides (do this in 2-3 batches) and remove meat and reserve.

Heat the remaining oil and add the onions along with a large pinch of salt. Cook over low heat for 6-7 minutes or until beginning to soften. Add the sugar, flour and vinegar and stir over high heat for 2-3 minutes. Pour the ale over and stir until it begins to boil.

Return the meat to the casserole and season it with salt and pepper. Cover the pan and place it in the oven. Cook the stew for 1 ½-2 hours, until the beef is very tender and the sauce has thickened. Serve immediately on warmed plates or cool and chill (covered) until ready to serve. Reheat gently over low heat (do not boil).

****

Chilli con Carne
(Serves 4)

This classic recipe couldn't be easier and it tastes even better the next day. Serve Chilli con Carne over boiled rice and encourage everyone to add chopped onion, soured cream and grated cheddar to taste. Or ladle Chilli over jacket potatoes and top with some grated cheese.

2 tablespoons olive oil

1 medium onion, chopped

1 clove garlic, chopped

450g beef mince, defrosted

400g tin chopped tomatoes

400g tin cooked kidney beans, drained

1 bay leaf

1-3 teaspoons chilli powder, according to taste

50ml dry red wine (optional)

Salt and pepper to taste

Chopped red onion, soured cream and grated cheddar cheese, to serve

Heat the olive oil in a large pan and add the chopped onion and garlic, along with a pinch of salt. Cook until soft. Add the mince to the pan and sauté, stirring, until the meat is broken into small clumps and is well cooked. Pour off any excess fat.

Add the tomatoes, beans, bay leaf and chilli powder to the pan, mixing well. Stir in the red wine, if using. Cover and simmer gently over very low heat for about 1 hour, stirring occasionally. The longer it cooks, the thicker it gets and the better it will taste.

Serve over rice in warmed bowls, passing the garnishes separately. Or cool and chill (covered), until ready to serve. Reheat the chilli over low heat, stirring occasionally, until it is piping hot.

****

CHICKEN

Spanish Chicken Stew
(Serves 4)

Garlicky chorizo and black olives add an unmistakably Spanish flavour to this stew. If you don't want to include potatoes, you can leave them out and add a tin of chick peas instead. Spanish Chicken Stew reheats well and tastes even better the next day. Serve it with crusty bread and a mixed salad.

2 tablespoons olive oil

4 chicken portions, defrosted

1 medium onion, chopped

1 garlic clove, finely minced

50g chorizo, cut into small pieces

50ml white wine

400g tin chopped tomatoes

1 teaspoon dried thyme

2 bay leaves

50ml water

1 chicken stock cube, crumbled

4 medium potatoes, cut into rough chunks

12 black olives, stoned and cut in half (optional)

Salt and ground black pepper, to taste

Heat the olive oil in a large saucepan over a medium heat, then brown the chicken all over (in two batches if necessary). Remove with a slotted spoon and reserve. Add the onion, garlic and a large pinch of salt to the pan and cook for 3-4 minutes, stirring, until softened and lightly browned.

Add the chorizo and cook for 3-4 minutes, stirring occasionally. Add the wine and reduce by half. Stir in the tomatoes, thyme, bay leaves, water and stock cube. Stir well to mix. Return the chicken to the pan. Cover and simmer gently for 20 minutes. Stir in the potatoes (or chick peas) and olives and cook for a further 35 minutes.

Serve immediately on warmed plates, or cool and chill until ready to serve. Reheat gently over low heat until stew is piping hot.

****

Chicken with Mustard Sauce
(Serves 4)

This classic French bistro dish is usually made with rabbit, but chicken makes a good substitute. Serve Chicken with Mustard Sauce with mashed potatoes or boiled rice to soak up all the rich, tangy sauce.

4 chicken portions, defrosted

100ml Dijon mustard

3 tablespoons olive oil

1 tablespoon butter

300ml dry white wine

250ml water

1 chicken stock cube, crumbled

1 large onion, finely chopped

1 tablespoon plain flour

1 teaspoon dried thyme

1 bay leaf

salt and pepper to taste

Brush one side of each chicken portion with mustard. Heat the olive oil and butter together in a large pan over medium heat. When the fat is hot, add the chicken portions mustard side down, and cook till brown (about 5 minutes). Do not crowd the pan; if necessary, brown the chicken in two batches.

Turn the chicken over and brush the browned side with additional mustard. Season with salt and pepper. Brown the uncooked sides of the chicken portions for another 5 minutes. Once both sides have been fully browned, transfer the chicken to a plate and reserve.

Add several tablespoons of the white wine to the pan and cook, stirring, while you scrape up any browned bits sticking to the bottom of the pan. Add the onions and cook, stirring, until golden brown (about 5 minutes). Remove the pan from the heat. Sprinkle the flour over the onions and stir to coat. Add the remaining wine, the water and the stock cube and stir well, then add the thyme and bay leaf.

Return the chicken to the pan. Bring to a simmer over medium heat and cook gently for about 45 minutes or until chicken is fully cooked and sauce has thickened. Season to taste with salt and ground black pepper, and serve on warmed plates.

****

Jambalaya
(Serves 4)

An authentic Creole speciality from New Orleans, Jambalaya makes a hearty one-dish meal. Like Paella, the recipe can vary but it always includes rice, meat and vegetables. Crusty bread and a green salad make the perfect accompaniments.

4 chicken portions, defrosted

4 tablespoons olive oil

1 medium onion, finely chopped

2 tomatoes, chopped

1 red pepper (seeds removed), chopped

2 sticks celery, chopped

250ml rice

750ml boiling water

2 chicken stock cubes, crumbled

1 bay leaf

1 teaspoon dried thyme

Hot sauce to taste (optional)

Salt and pepper to taste

100g cooked ham or chorizo, finely chopped

Heat the olive oil in a pan and brown the chicken portions thoroughly on all sides. Remove the browned chicken from the pan and set aside.

Add onion and tomatoes to the hot oil in the pan and sauté for 3 minutes, stirring frequently. Stir in the red pepper, celery and rice. When the rice is well coated with oil, return the chicken to the pan. Stir in the boiling water, crumbled stock cubes, bay leaf and thyme.

Cover the pan and simmer gently over low heat until the chicken is tender and the rice nearly cooked (this should take 15-20 minutes). Mix the chopped ham or chorizo into the rice. Dry out the jambalaya by placing it (uncovered) in a 170 degree C oven for 5-10 minutes. Serve immediately on warmed plates.

****

Chicken Adobo
(Serves 4)

Most Filipino cooks have a family recipe for Chicken Adobo. Although the spices may vary, the dish always includes vinegar and soy sauce; that combination is what gives Chicken Adobo its rich and subtle flavour. Try it with boiled rice – although the sauce is an unusual one, you'll find that it gives chicken a whole new appeal.

4 chicken portions, defrosted
4 garlic cloves, coarsely chopped
1 tablespoon vegetable oil
120ml vinegar
60ml soy sauce
1/2 teaspoon ground black pepper
1 bay leaf

Heat the oil in a large frying pan over medium-high heat. Brown the chicken on all sides in two batches, about 8 minutes for each batch. Remove chicken and reserve.

Pour off all but 1 tablespoon fat from the pan, and cook garlic over low heat in the remaining fat, stirring until golden. Add vinegar, soy sauce, pepper and bay leaf and stir.

Return chicken to the pan, along with any juices, and simmer, covered, for 15 minutes. Remove the lid and simmer over low heat, turning chicken occasionally, until the sauce has thickened enough to coat the chicken, about 15 minutes. Serve immediately, on warmed plates.

Note: Do not add any salt to this dish, as the soy sauce is sufficiently salty.

****

Country Captain
(Serves 4)

No one is quite sure how this chicken stew got its name, but one theory is that curry powder, one of its key ingredients, was first brought to Savannah, Georgia by a 19th century British sea captain. Since that time, Country Captain has been a firm favourite in the American South, and there are lots of regional variations. Like all stews, it benefits from being made in advance and refrigerated overnight before serving. Serve with boiled rice and additional chutney, if desired.

4 chicken portions, defrosted

125g smoked streaky bacon, cut into 1cm pieces

2 tablespoons olive oil

30g plain flour

Salt and ground black pepper, to taste

1 medium onion, chopped

1 green pepper, cored, seeded and chopped

2 cloves garlic, finely minced

2 tablespoons curry powder

1 teaspoon dried thyme

400g tin tomatoes

500ml water

2 chicken stock cubes, crumbled

2 tablespoons chutney

2 tablespoons sultanas or raisins

In a large pan, brown the bacon over medium heat. Remove the bacon from the pan and reserve. Season the flour with salt and pepper and coat the chicken on all sides with the flour (shake off excess). Brown the chicken on all sides in the bacon fat over medium high heat. Remove the chicken from the pan and reserve.

Add the 2 tablespoons of olive oil to the pan along with the onions, green pepper and a pinch of salt. Cook over low heat for 10 minutes, stirring occasionally, until softened. Add the garlic and cook for 2 minutes longer, stirring. Sprinkle with the curry powder and thyme and cook 1 minute longer, stirring.

Add the tomatoes, water, stock cubes and chutney to pan and stir until well mixed. Return the reserved bacon and chicken to the pan and bring to the boil. Reduce the heat to medium and simmer for 30 minutes, adding the sultanas during the last 5 minutes of cooking time. Serve with boiled rice and additional chutney, if desired.

****

Chicken Cacciatore
(Serves 4)

This rustic Italian dish is perfect for a family supper. Cacciatore means Hunter's Style and whilst there are many variations of this dish, onion, garlic, tomatoes and wine always form the basis of the sauce. My version of Chicken Cacciatore includes extra vegetables, but if you don't have them in the fridge, simply leave them out – the dish will be just as nice without them.

4 chicken portions, defrosted

2 tablespoons olive oil

1 medium onion, very thinly sliced

150ml white wine

2 cloves garlic, very finely chopped

1 stalk celery, thinly sliced

1 green pepper, cored, seeded and cut into thin strips

1 carrot, thinly sliced

400g tin chopped tomatoes

Salt and pepper, to taste

In a large pan, heat 1 tablespoon of the olive oil and brown the chicken portions on all sides over medium-high heat. Remove the browned chicken to a plate.

Pour the remaining tablespoon of oil into the pan and add the onion. Cook, stirring, over medium-high heat until the onion is golden brown. Add the wine and let it bubble for about 30 seconds, whilst scraping up the browned bits on the bottom of the pan.

Add the garlic, celery, green pepper, carrot and tomatoes and stir well to mix. Return the chicken pieces to the pan and spoon the sauce over them. Reduce the heat to low and cover the pan. Simmer for 45-50 minutes or until the chicken juices run clear and the meat is tender. Add salt and pepper to taste and serve immediately on warmed plates.

This dish reheats well and can be made in advance. Store covered, in the fridge. Reheat gently in a covered pan, turning the chicken portions until they are piping hot.

****

Stuffed Chicken Breasts
(Serves 6)

Here are two versions of a dish that is simple to prepare but impressive enough to serve to guests. It's also a good way to use up leftovers: if you've got a bit of mayonnaise or cheese and a few rashers of bacon, you can turn plain chicken breasts into something special. Stuffed Chicken Breasts are also delicious chilled – slice them crossways to show off the filling.

6 chicken breasts, boneless and skinless, defrosted
6 rashers of streaky bacon (or slices of Parma ham)
1 portion of either Greek or French filling (recipes below)

To make Stuffed Chicken Breasts: heat the oven to 180 degrees C. Cut a horizontal slit in each chicken breast to create a pocket for the filling (do not cut all the way through). Season the chicken with salt and ground black pepper. Stuff each chicken breast with $1/6^{th}$ of your selected filling mixture.

Wrap each chicken breast with the bacon (or Parma ham) by spiraling it tightly around the stuffed breast, tucking the ends underneath. Place the chicken breasts in a roasting tin. (The dish can be prepared to this point and then refrigerated for a few hours, if desired.) Roast at 180 degrees for 45-50 minutes or until the chicken and bacon are thoroughly cooked.

Greek filling:

50ml mayonnaise
1 garlic clove, finely minced
50g feta cheese, crumbled
½ bag spinach, cooked and drained

Mix the mayonnaise, garlic and feta in a bowl. Place the cooked spinach in a sieve and press down on it firmly, to remove all the liquid. Chop the spinach finely and stir it into the mayonnaise mixture, mixing thoroughly.

French filling:

1 leek, white part only, rinsed well and finely minced
25g butter
100g soft goat cheese

Melt the butter in a medium pan over medium heat. Add the leek and a large pinch of salt and cook, stirring, until leek is soft but not browned. Remove from heat and cool slightly. Stir the leek mixture into the goat cheese until thoroughly combined.

****

Greek Chicken with Oregano
(Serves 4)

This rustic dish has loads of flavour and it couldn't be simpler to make. Don't reduce the amount of oregano – although it looks like a lot, it is essential to the success of the dish. If you've got room in your tin, you can roast potatoes alongside the chicken. Cut medium potatoes into quarters and parboil them for 10-15 minutes, then add them to the tin before it goes into the oven. Stir well so they are coated with the oil and lemon mixture. Arrange the potatoes in a single layer and make sure that they don't cover the chicken. They will be ready when the chicken is cooked.

4 chicken portions, defrosted

3 tablespoons olive oil

1 clove garlic, finely minced

1 tablespoon dried oregano, crumbled

Juice of 1 lemon

Salt and ground black pepper, to taste

Preheat the oven to 200 degrees C. Place the chicken pieces in a large roasting tin and drizzle over the olive oil. Distribute the chopped garlic and oregano evenly over the chicken, then squeeze the lemon juice over everything. Sprinkle salt and pepper over the chicken pieces, to taste. Roast for 40-45 minutes, or until the skin is browned and crispy and the juices run clear.

FISH AND SEAFOOD

Roast Salmon with Garlic and Mustard
(Serves 2, recipe can be doubled)

In this recipe, tangy Dijon mustard complements the richness of salmon. Oven roasted salmon has a lovely texture and it is equally good served hot or cold, at a dinner party or a picnic. Any leftovers can be flaked and added to cooked pasta, along with some cooked peas and warmed cream (or Greek yoghurt).

2 frozen salmon fillets, defrosted

1 clove garlic, finely minced

2 teaspoons Dijon mustard

Preheat oven to 200 degrees C. Place the salmon in a roasting tin and spread half the mustard evenly onto each fillet. Sprinkle with the garlic and roast for 15-20 minutes, or until the salmon is just cooked through.

Serve immediately on warmed plates or cool and chill (covered) until ready to serve.

Oriental Salmon
(Serves 2, recipe can be doubled)

This dish is actually quite flexible: if you don't have salmon, you can use prawns. The vegetables can also vary according to season or personal preference. I usually include mushrooms, spring onions and broccoli, but green beans, asparagus, mangetout, bean sprouts, spinach, celery and carrots are equally good. Serve with boiled rice to soak up all the lovely sauce.

2 frozen salmon fillets, defrosted

2 tablespoons olive oil

1 clove garlic, finely minced

1 tablespoon finely minced fresh ginger

Hot pepper sauce, to taste (optional)

Fresh vegetables for two: mushrooms, broccoli, green beans, etc., all cut into bite-sized pieces

125ml water

1 chicken stock cube, crumbled

1 tablespoon soy sauce

Boiled rice for two, to serve

Heat the olive oil in a large pan over medium-high heat (use a pan with a tight-fitting lid). Add the garlic and ginger and cook for 1 minute, stirring occasionally. Add the vegetables all at once and stir to coat with the oil.

Pour over the water, soy sauce and hot pepper sauce (if using), add the stock cube and mix well. Place the salmon fillets on top of the vegetables. Put the lid on the pan and cook over medium heat for 10-12 minutes.

Check to see that the fish is cooked through. Serve immediately on warmed plates, with the fish and vegetables arranged around the rice and the cooking juices poured over.

****

Mackerel with Horseradish Cream Lentils
(Serves 4)

In this recipe, a tangy horseradish sauce balances the richness of the mackerel. Mackerel with Horseradish Cream Lentils is a hearty dish that needs no accompaniment other than a steamed green vegetable. If mackerel fillets aren't available, defrosted salmon fillets can be used instead – they make a fine substitute.

1 tablespoon butter

1 tablespoon olive oil

1 onion, finely chopped

2 cloves garlic, finely chopped

375ml dried lentils

1 teaspoon dried thyme

450ml water

2 chicken stock cubes, crumbled

2 tablespoons horseradish sauce

75ml double cream

Juice of ½ lemon

Salt and pepper, to taste

4 mackerel fillets

Heat the oven to 180 degrees. In a medium saucepan, heat the butter and olive oil. Add the onion and cook for 5 minutes, until softened but not browned. Add the garlic, cook for one minute, then stir in the lentils, thyme, water and stock cubes. Bring to the boil and transfer to an ovenproof dish. Cover the dish with a lid (or tin foil) and place in the oven; cook for 20 minutes.

Remove the lentils from the oven, stir in the horseradish sauce, cream and lemon juice. Season the mackerel fillets and place them on top of the lentil mixture. Return the dish to the oven and cook, covered, for 10 minutes or until fish is opaque and flakes easily with a fork. Serve immediately on warmed plates, placing each fillet on a bed of lentils.

****

Mackerel and Tomatoes in Wine Sauce
(Serves 4)

A familiar fish in an elegant guise. Serve Mackerel and Tomatoes in Wine Sauce with a simple green vegetable and some boiled rice to catch the delicious sauce.

2 tablespoons butter

2 tablespoons plain flour

1 teaspoon dried basil (or mixed herbs)

Salt and pepper, to taste

125ml double cream

125ml white wine

4 mackerel fillets

3 tomatoes, sliced

Melt the butter in a saucepan; stir in the flour, basil and seasonings. Slowly add the liquids (cream first and then wine) and continue to cook over low heat, stirring constantly, until the sauce is smooth and thickened.

Heat the oven to 180 degrees. Lay the mackerel fillets in an ovenproof dish, place the tomato slices on top of them and pour over the wine sauce. Cook for 30 minutes, or until the fish is opaque and flakes easily with a fork. Serve immediately, on warmed plates.

Spicy Grilled Mackerel with Beetroot Salsa
(Serves 4)

This simple dish is packed with flavour and it makes a colourful main course, especially when served with lightly steamed spinach. The Salsa can be made in advance and kept chilled, so it's ready when you return with the catch of the day.

4 medium beetroot, cooked and diced into small cubes

1 eating apple, peeled, cored and diced into small cubes

3 spring onions, thinly sliced

Juice of ½ lemon

2 tablespoons olive oil

Salt and pepper, to taste

4 mackerel fillets

1 teaspoon curry powder

Additional olive oil, for drizzling

Start with the Salsa: combine the beetroot, apple, spring onions, lemon juice and olive oil in a bowl and season to taste. Set it aside (or chill until needed) whilst you prepare the fish.

Heat the grill and cover the rack with foil. Season the mackerel fillets to taste and sprinkle evenly with the curry powder. Drizzle over a bit of olive oil, and rub the oil and curry powder into the fish. Grill for 5 minutes or until the skin is crisp and the fish is opaque and flakes easily with a fork. Serve immediately, accompanied by the Salsa.

Salmon with Red Wine Sauce
(Serves 4)

Fish with red wine is an unusual combination, but this sauce complements the richness (and colour) of the salmon beautifully.

4 frozen salmon fillets, defrosted
1 tablespoon olive oil
350ml dry red wine
2 tablespoons ground black pepper
2 tablespoons finely grated fresh ginger
2 tablespoons finely minced garlic
40g butter (cold)
Salt, to taste

Season the salmon with salt. Heat the olive oil in a large frying pan over medium-high heat and sear the salmon on both sides until golden (2-3 minutes total cooking time). Add the wine, pepper, ginger and garlic to the pan. Cook the salmon at a gentle simmer, turning fillets over once, until just cooked through (5-6 minutes total).

Transfer the fish to 4 heated plates and keep warm, covered. Cut the butter into 3 pieces. Boil the wine mixture rapidly until syrupy and reduced to about 75ml. Remove the pan from the heat and add the butter piece by piece, stirring until the sauce is smooth and well mixed. Season the sauce to taste and pour over the salmon fillets.

Cod with Parma Ham & Spicy Sauce
(Serves 2, recipe can be doubled)

One of the simplest fish dishes I know, but impressive enough for a dinner party. If cod isn't available, any white fish will do. Make sure you don't overcook the fish; if you remove it from the heat just before the interior becomes opaque, it will continue to cook to moist perfection whilst waiting to be served.

4 small frozen cod fillets, defrosted

Juice of 1 lemon

4 slices Parma ham

1 tablespoon olive oil

3 tablespoons mayonnaise (regular or low fat)

1 clove garlic, kept whole but crushed to release its juices

1 teaspoon chilli powder or a few drops of hot pepper sauce

Start by making the Spicy Mayonnaise: Stir the crushed garlic and chilli powder (or hot pepper sauce) into the mayonnaise and mix well. Set aside until ready to serve.

Sprinkle each fillet with lemon juice and then wrap it in a slice of Parma ham. Heat the olive oil in a large frying pan and add the wrapped fish fillets. Fry for 6-8 minutes, turning once. Remove the garlic clove from the Spicy Mayonnaise. Serve the fish fillets, two per person, on warmed plates, topped with a spoonful of the mayonnaise.

Prawns with Feta
(Serves 2, recipe can be doubled)

This quick and easy dish is filled with bright Mediterranean flavours. Add a green salad and some crusty bread, and you'll have dinner on the table in less than half an hour.

250g frozen cooked prawns, defrosted

1 clove garlic, minced

1 tablespoon olive oil

400g tin chopped tomatoes

1/2 teaspoon dried thyme

10 black olives, stoned and chopped

50g feta cheese, crumbled

Ground black pepper, to taste

Cooked pasta or rice, to serve two people

Heat the olive oil in a saucepan and briefly sauté the garlic in the oil. Add the tomatoes, thyme and olives and simmer mixture for 10 minutes, stirring occasionally. Stir in the prawns and heat for no more than 3 minutes, just enough to warm the prawns through (longer cooking will toughen them). Remove the pan from the heat and stir in the feta cheese. Add ground black pepper to taste (you shouldn't need any salt as the olives and cheese are both salty). Serve over cooked pasta or rice.

More ideas for fish and seafood:

Add 250g cooked prawns to Jambalaya (page 44), at the point when you add the ham.

Roast salmon with Tzatziki (page 96)

Grilled Fish with Honey Mustard Vinaigrette (page 98)

Roast Fish with Tomato and Feta Topping (page 130)

Roast Salmon with Hummus (page 131)

Teriyaki Mackerel or Salmon (page 138)

PASTA AND PIZZA

If you have pasta, olive oil and garlic in your store cupboard, you have the makings of a feast. Add a tin of tomatoes and a bit of oregano to the mix and you've got a dish full of Mediterranean sunshine. Capers, olives and anchovies will lend zest. If you'd like a bit more substance, throw in some tuna or chopped vegetables.

With a little creativity, you can easily create your own 'house special' pasta. Use the recipes in this chapter as inspiration, but don't feel limited by them – almost any meat, vegetable or cheese can be the basis for a fantastic pasta sauce. How about strips of chicken breast sautéed with olive oil and garlic? Or a tin of beans mixed with chopped tomatoes and olives, topped with grated cheese? Don't forget about leftovers – roast vegetables or meats can be chopped into bits and blended with olive oil (or a creamy sauce) for a quick and easy meal.

Pizza is equally versatile – a simple flour-and-milk mixture becomes the base for almost any topping you can imagine. For a Greek-style pizza, try feta cheese, prawns and olives. Garlicky cooked spinach and Brie also make a wonderful combination. In fact, almost anything goes…

Pasta with Blue Cheese and Spinach
(Serves 4)

Rich, creamy and full of flavour, this simple vegetarian pasta should please everyone.

1 bag of leaf spinach, washed and drained
500g fettuccine, tagliatelle or spaghetti
225g blue cheese, crumbled
90ml milk
25g butter
Ground black pepper, to taste

Place the spinach in a large saucepan with just the water clinging to the leaves after washing. Cook, stirring, over medium-high heat for 2-3 minutes, until just wilted. Drain well in a colander or sieve, pressing out the excess liquid. Chop the drained spinach coarsely.

Cook the pasta according to label directions. While the pasta is cooking, place the blue cheese, milk and butter in a medium saucepan and heat over low heat, stirring constantly, until it becomes a creamy sauce. Stir in the drained spinach and season to taste with black pepper. Drain the pasta and mix with the sauce. Serve immediately on warmed plates.

Summer Pasta
(Serves 6)

This uncooked sauce is perfect for a summer evening, when you want to linger outdoors as long as possible. Summer Pasta makes an excellent vegetarian main, or you can serve it as an accompaniment to grilled meat or fish. If you'd like to add a bit of protein to this dish, sprinkle some crumbled feta cheese over the pasta before serving.

6 ripe tomatoes, cored and chopped
1 green pepper, pared and chopped
½ cucumber, peeled and chopped
1 teaspoon salt
1 teaspoon ground black pepper
125ml olive oil
3 spring onions, chopped
1 clove garlic, finely minced
1 teaspoon dried oregano or mixed herbs, crumbled
500g dried pasta shapes such as penne or shells
Feta cheese (if desired)

Combine the tomatoes (and their juices), green pepper, cucumber, salt, pepper and olive oil in a medium-sized bowl; mix gently. Add the spring onions, garlic and herbs, and mix again. Cover the bowl and leave it at room temperature for 1-2 hours, so the flavours can blend. (Do not refrigerate the sauce during this time, or the tomatoes will not blend properly with the other ingredients.)

Cook the pasta according to label directions, until just tender. Drain the pasta and transfer it to a large warmed bowl. Add the sauce mixture and mix gently until the pasta is well coated. Sprinkle with feta, if using, and serve immediately on warmed plates.

****

Pasta al Pesto
(Serves 2, recipe can be doubled)

Pasta al Pesto is the creation of Patrizia Fursdon, who grew up in Italy and now works in the Lundy shop. This recipe demonstrates her creative approach to cookery, which uses 'leftovers' to produce a memorable main course. Pasta al Pesto is extremely flexible – if you don't have broccoli or mushrooms (or don't like them), simply leave them out. As for which pasta to use, Patrizia says: 'Any pasta shape and any jar of pesto can be used to achieve amazing results, as long as you use your imagination. Buon appetito!'

80-100g pasta per person

2 teaspoons green pesto (or more, according to taste)

1 medium potato, peeled and chopped into small cubes

A small quantity of uncooked broccoli, chopped into bite-sized pieces

1 tablespoon olive oil (extra-virgin, if available)

Uncooked mushrooms, sliced

1 clove garlic, finely minced

White wine (if desired)

Salt and ground black pepper, to taste

Ham or salami, chopped into small bits (if desired)

Parmesan, cheddar or any other hard cheese, grated

Bring a large pot of water to the boil over high heat. To improve the texture and taste of the pasta, boil the potato cubes for 5-10 minutes before adding the pasta to the water. Follow the cooking instructions on the packet of pasta, but always taste it to be sure it is cooked to perfection, i.e., in the way you like it (neither too hard nor overcooked). To cook the broccoli, add it to the boiling water along with the pasta. But since it only needs to be cooked for 5-7 minutes, you should add it towards the end of the pasta cooking time.

While the pasta, potato and broccoli are cooking, heat the olive oil in a separate pan with the finely chopped garlic. Add the sliced mushrooms, a little water (or even better, some white wine), salt and black pepper, to taste, and cook for 5-10 minutes. If you don't have any mushrooms, Patrizia suggests that you ask in the shop if they have any old ones that you can have for free (there are always some in the shop's back room). Then, with a little patience, peel away the top layer and check that they are edible underneath. To make your mushrooms tastier, you can add some chopped ham or salami to the same pan. Sauté the meat along with the mushrooms, stirring, until the mushrooms are cooked.

When everything is ready, drain the pasta well (toss it in the air several times and catch it again in the colander). Return the drained pasta and vegetables to the pasta cooking pan, add the mushrooms and the pesto, and mix well over very low heat. Remember that you need very little pesto to achieve the best results! Serve on warmed plates, sprinkled with grated cheese.

Easy Pizza
(Serves 4)

With nothing more than self-raising flour and a little milk, you can make a quick pizza base that can be topped with almost anything from the fridge. Even though this recipe calls for chorizo and cheddar cheese, feel free to substitute cooked chicken, bacon or ham and any cheese you've got in the house. Suggestions for vegetarian toppings include: mushrooms, olives, capers, broccoli and red peppers. Use your imagination – almost anything goes!

2 tablespoons olive oil

½ onion, finely chopped

1 clove garlic, finely minced

Pinch of salt

400g tin chopped tomatoes

1 teaspoon dried oregano

Ground black pepper

400ml self-raising flour

200ml milk

Large pinch of salt

Olive oil (to grease tins)

1 tablespoon tomato puree

200ml grated cheddar cheese

6 slices chorizo (cut into quarters)

8 olives, stoned and halved

2 teaspoons dried oregano

Preheat oven to 200 degrees C. Start with the tomato sauce: heat the 2 tablespoons of olive oil in a saucepan over medium heat. Add the onion, garlic and a pinch of salt and cook until onion softens (about 3 minutes). Add the tomatoes and oregano, bring to the boil, then reduce the heat and simmer uncovered for 15 minutes or until reduced to half of its original volume, stirring occasionally.

While the sauce is reducing, prepare the pizza bases. Pour 1 tablespoon of olive oil into each of the two sandwich tins and spread evenly. In a large bowl, mix the flour, milk and a generous pinch of salt. Using a large spoon, stir the flour and milk together until it forms a sticky dough. Split the dough into two equal halves and press each half into an oiled sandwich tin. Flipping the dough over several times, press it firmly to the edges of the tin, making sure that both the top and bottom of the dough are well oiled.

Spread ½ tablespoon of tomato puree onto each pizza base, all the way to the edge. Place the bases in the hot oven to rise for 10 minutes.

Add a large pinch of ground black pepper to the reduced tomato sauce. Remove the risen bases from the oven and divide the sauce between them, spreading it evenly. Top the sauce with the grated cheddar, chorizo and olives, then sprinkle each pizza with 1 teaspoon of oregano. Place the pizzas back in the oven for 15-20 minutes or until the cheese is bubbling and beginning to brown.

Cold Noodles with Spicy Peanut Sauce
(Serves 4)

Pasta came originally from China, and variations of this Chinese noodle dish can be found on restaurant menus all over the world. It is easy to make and because it needs to be prepared in advance, it makes an ideal summer meal.

250g spaghetti or fine egg noodles, cooked according to label directions and drained

3 tablespoons vegetable oil

2 tablespoons peanut butter

2 tablespoons soy sauce

1 tablespoon water

1 teaspoon sugar

3 spring onions, chopped

1 teaspoon grated fresh ginger

Hot pepper sauce, to taste (optional)

½ cucumber, peeled, seeded and cut into thin slivers

Mix the noodles with 1 tablespoon of the oil, coating them well. In another large bowl, combine the remaining oil, peanut butter, soy sauce, water, sugar, spring onions, ginger and hot pepper sauce (if using). Stir until well blended and creamy. Add the noodles to the sauce, mix gently until they are well coated. Top the noodle mixture with the cucumber slivers and chill for at least one hour. Serve cold or at room temperature.

VEGETARIAN MAINS

Spinach and Chick Pea Stew
(Serves 4)

This rustic stew evokes the exotic flavours of North Africa. It is quick and easy to prepare and makes a satisfying lunch or family supper. Ladle it over couscous or serve with some crusty bread or a stack of warm pitta.

1 onion, chopped

2 tablespoons olive oil

3 cloves garlic, finely chopped

1 teaspoon ground cinnamon

400g tin chopped tomatoes

2 400g tins chick peas, drained

200ml water

1 vegetable stock cube, crumbled

350g spinach, washed and shredded

Handful of sultanas

Handful of cashews, chopped

Salt and pepper, to taste

Heat the olive oil in a large pan; add the onion, garlic and cinnamon. Cook over low heat, stirring, until golden (10 minutes). Add the tomatoes, chick peas, water and stock cube. Stir well and bring to the boil. Cover, reduce heat and cook for 20 minutes. Stir in the spinach and sultanas and cook for 5 minutes. Stir in the nuts, season to taste & serve.

Potato and Leek Gratin
(Serves 4-6)

This traditional French country dish takes a bit of time to prepare, but once it is bubbling away in the oven you can relax with a glass of wine and a book. This gratin goes well with bread and cheese and a green salad.

30g butter

1 medium onion, finely chopped

4 medium leeks, white part only, well rinsed and finely chopped

4 large baking potatoes, peeled and very thinly sliced

125ml water

1 vegetable stock cube, crumbled

125ml dry white wine

1 teaspoon dried thyme

Salt and ground black pepper, to taste

Preheat the oven to 190 degrees C. Melt the butter in a large frying pan. Add the onions, leeks and a large pinch of salt and cook, covered, over low heat until they are soft (about 10 minutes).

Add the potatoes and mix well. Add the water, stock cube, wine, thyme and continue to cook, covered, over medium heat for another 15 minutes. Add salt and pepper to taste, and transfer the mixture to a large baking dish.

Place the dish in the oven and cook, uncovered, until the potatoes are soft and golden on top and most of the liquid has been absorbed (50-60 minutes). Serve immediately on warmed plates.

****

Provencal Vegetable Stew
(Serves 4)

With its topping of spicy rouille, this lovely stew hints at bouillabaisse, but it is entirely vegetarian. I've provided an easy recipe for a Mock Rouille (page 95), which is based on ready-made mayonnaise. Pass the rouille round the table - a spoonful stirred into Provencal Vegetable Stew turns this simple dish into a rich and flavoursome meal.

3 tablespoons olive oil

2 large leeks, rinsed well and sliced into rings

1 tablespoon grated fresh ginger

1 strip of orange zest

2 bay leaves

1 litre water

3 vegetable stock cubes, crumbled

3 medium potatoes, chopped into bite-sized chunks

1 red pepper, cored, seeded and chopped into bite-sized pieces

1 medium courgette or 150ml green beans, trimmed and chopped into bite-sized pieces

8 medium mushrooms, halved

400g tin red kidney beans, drained

Salt and ground black pepper, to taste

Mock Rouille, to serve

Heat the oil in a large pan over medium heat. Add the leeks, ginger, orange zest and bay leaves and cook for 3 minutes. Add the water, stock cubes and potatoes. Increase the heat and bring the mixture to the boil, stirring to dissolve the stock cubes. Reduce the heat and simmer gently for 10 minutes, or until the potatoes are almost tender.

Add the red pepper, courgettes (or green beans), mushrooms, and kidney beans. Cover and simmer gently for 10-15 minutes or until all the vegetables are tender but not too soft. Season to taste. Serve in warmed soup bowls, passing the rouille separately.

****

Mushroom Stroganoff
(Serves 4)

Mushrooms are the star of this dish, which is loosely based on the classic Beef Stroganoff. Quick and easy to prepare, Mushroom Stroganoff is special enough to serve to guests. If you fancy a change from pasta, you can serve this rich dish over boiled rice, jacket potatoes or even toast.

1 tablespoon butter

2 garlic cloves, finely minced

1 large onion, chopped

900g mushrooms, cleaned and sliced

1 tablespoon plain flour

60ml dry white wine

120ml soured cream

Salt and ground black pepper, to taste

500g freshly cooked and drained pasta

Melt the butter in a large pan over medium-high heat. Add the garlic, onion and a large pinch of salt and cook, stirring, for 2-3 minutes or until softened. Add the mushrooms and cook until tender and most of the liquid has evaporated, about 10 minutes.

Reduce the heat to medium and add the flour. Cook, stirring constantly, for one minute. Add the wine and cook until the mixture thickens, stirring frequently, about 3 minutes. Remove the pan from the heat and mix in the soured cream, then season to taste with salt and pepper. If serving with pasta, mix the pasta well with the mushroom mixture and serve immediately, on warmed plates.

****

Risotto with Green Beans and Pesto
(Serves 2, recipe can be doubled)

This simple recipe is deceptively delicious. Risotto with Green Beans and Pesto makes a lovely special dinner for two or the recipe can be doubled to serve guests. If green beans aren't available, peas make a very good substitute.

1 litre water

2 vegetable stock cubes, crumbled

1 small onion, finely chopped

1 tablespoon olive oil

350ml Arborio rice

250g fresh or frozen green beans, cut into thin slices

4 tablespoons pesto

2 tomatoes, chopped

125ml grated Parmesan

Bring the water to the boil and stir in the stock cubes. Cover the pan and reduce the heat so that the stock continues to simmer.

In a large saucepan, heat the oil and cook the onion until it has softened (about 5 minutes). Do not let it brown. Add the rice and stir to coat it with oil. Ladle about 200ml of stock into the pan and stir it into the rice. When the rice has absorbed the stock, stir in another 200ml of stock and cook until it is absorbed. Repeat this step until you have about 400ml of stock remaining.

At this point, add the green beans and cook them with the rice for a couple of minutes. Then continue to add stock, allowing it to absorb as before, until the rice and green beans are cooked al dente. Total cooking time should be about 20 minutes.

Remove the rice and beans from the heat, stir in the pesto, tomatoes and Parmesan, and serve immediately, on warmed plates.

****

Vegetable Biryani
(Serves 6)

Vegetable Biryani is perfect for an informal dinner with friends. It can be prepared in advance and then chilled, ready to go into the oven when dinnertime approaches. This hearty dish needs few accompaniments – perhaps a shredded carrot salad and some cooling Cucumber Raita (page 94) for added colour and contrast.

400ml rice

1 tablespoon vegetable or olive oil

2 vegetable stock cubes, crumbled

800ml boiling water

1 medium onion, chopped

2 tablespoons vegetable or olive oil

2 teaspoons grated fresh ginger

1 teaspoon cinnamon

1 teaspoon curry powder

Hot pepper sauce, to taste

125ml water

1 medium carrot, chopped

½ cauliflower, divided into small florets

1 medium green pepper, chopped

1 tomato, chopped

120ml peas (fresh or frozen)

150ml raisins or sultanas

400g tin chick peas, drained

Salt to taste

To garnish: toasted cashews (or other nuts), plain yoghurt, quartered hard-boiled eggs and chutney

Start by cooking the rice: heat the oil in a large saucepan over medium-high heat and add the rice, stirring to coat each kernel. Add the boiling water and stock cubes, stirring to make sure the cubes dissolve completely. Return the mixture to the boil, cover the pan and reduce the heat. Simmer for 15-20 minutes or until the rice is cooked.

While the rice is cooking, prepare the vegetables. Heat the oil in a pan and add the onions along with a pinch of salt. Cook for 5 minutes, stirring occasionally. Mix in the ginger, cinnamon and curry powder and cook for 1 minute longer, stirring constantly. Add the 125ml water, hot pepper sauce (if using), carrot and cauliflower. Cover the pan and cook on low heat for 3-4 minutes. Stir in the green pepper, tomato, peas, raisins or sultanas and chick peas. Continue to simmer until the vegetables are barely tender, adding a little more water if necessary to prevent sticking. Add salt to taste.

Grease a large baking dish with butter or oil and spread half the rice in the bottom. Top with the vegetable mixture and then cover the vegetables with the remaining rice. Cover the dish tightly with aluminium foil and bake at 180 degrees for about 30 minutes (bake for one hour if the dish has been refrigerated). Serve the garnishes with the biryani, allowing each person to add them to his or her taste.

Other vegetarian main courses include:

Greek Pasta Salad (page 18)

Indian-style Lamb with Aubergine (substituting vegetables for the lamb) (page 28)

Pasta with Blue Cheese and Spinach (page 67)

Cold Noodles with Spicy Peanut Sauce (page 74)

Ratatouille (page 88)

Roasted Root Vegetables (page 92)

VEGETABLES

Stir Fried Vegetables
(Serves 2, recipe can be doubled)

Stir frying is an easy way to add extra flavour to vegetables, either fresh or frozen. Almost any vegetable can be stir fried, and I often make more than I need because the leftovers make excellent additions to salads.

1 tablespoon olive oil

1 clove garlic, finely minced

Enough vegetables for two: green beans, spinach, broccoli or whatever you fancy

2 teaspoons soy sauce

50ml water

Cut the green beans, broccoli and any other large vegetables into bite-sized pieces. Heat the olive oil in a large pan and add the garlic. Cook, stirring constantly, for 1 minute. Add the vegetables and cook, stirring, until they are coated with oil. Add the soy sauce and water, bring to the boil and cover. Reduce the heat and cook for 5-7 minutes or until vegetables are tender but still have some bite. Serve immediately or cool and chill for use in a salad.

Ratatouille
(Serves 4-5)

This is a simplified version of the Provencal classic, which normally requires all the vegetables to be cooked separately. Ratatouille can be served hot or cold as a vegetable, mixed with hot pasta as a sauce or used as a topping for grilled fish or chicken. It also makes a good topping for jacket potatoes.

1 medium aubergine, peeled and chopped into 2cm cubes

400g tin tomatoes, drained

2 green peppers, seeded and cut into 1cm wide strips

2 courgettes, chopped into 2cm cubes

1 onion, thinly sliced

2 cloves garlic, finely minced

3 tablespoons olive oil

Salt and ground black pepper to taste

125ml water

Combine all the vegetables in a large shallow pan. Sprinkle with the olive oil, salt and pepper. Add the water, cover the pan and cook over very low heat until the vegetables are tender, about 1 hour. Stir gently from time to time to prevent sticking. Cool and chill if serving cold.

Hasselback Potatoes
(Serves 4)

Originally from Sweden, this simple recipe is impressive enough to serve to guests. With their crispy exteriors, Hasselback Potatoes make a good alternative to roast potatoes. Serve them with a Sunday roast or grilled meats.

4 baking potatoes

1 teaspoon salt

40g butter, melted

2-3 teaspoons dried herbs of your choice (thyme, rosemary and mixed herbs are all good)

4 tablespoons grated cheddar or other hard cheese

Preheat the oven to 220 degrees C. Scrub the potatoes well. Using a sharp knife, cut them crossways into thin slices, but DO NOT cut all the way through the potato – stop about 1 cm from the bottom. Place the potatoes in a baking dish and fan them out slightly, Sprinkle evenly with the salt and dried herbs and drizzle with the melted butter.

Bake the potatoes for about 50 minutes. Remove them from the oven and sprinkle evenly with the grated cheese. Return them to the oven for another 10-15 minutes, until lightly browned and soft inside (check with a fork). Serve immediately.

Potato Gratin with Cheese and Ham
(Serves 4-6)

This simple dish originated in the French Alps, where they know all about cold weather. It makes a hearty winter supper, and it can be put together very quickly, leaving the cook free to enjoy a glass of red wine in front of the fire. Although the recipe calls for Gruyere cheese and smoked ham, feel free to substitute whatever cheese and cured meat you have in the fridge.

Cheddar or blue cheese combine well with cooked bacon in this dish, and goat cheese is lovely with Parma ham. If you use a crumbly cheese such as goat or blue rather than one that melts easily, you may want to pour 100ml of cream over everything before baking to ensure that the gratin doesn't dry out.

125g smoked ham (or other cured meat)

60g butter

4 large baking potatoes, peeled and very thinly sliced

250g Gruyere (or other) cheese, grated

Salt and pepper to taste

Preheat the oven to 190 degrees C. Cut the ham into 2cm wide strips. If you are using bacon, cook it and then cut it into strips.

Use 15g of the butter to grease a baking dish. Arrange half of the potatoes in a single layer in the dish. Lay half of the ham strips over the potatoes, and sprinkle half the cheese over the ham. Season with salt and pepper.

Repeat the potato, ham and cheese layers, ending with grated cheese. Cut the remaining butter into bits and dot the top of the gratin evenly with the butter bits. Bake, uncovered, until the gratin is golden, about 50 minutes. Take care not to overcook, as the gratin will dry out. Serve immediately on warmed plates.

****

Roasted Root Vegetables
(Serves 4)

Roasting brings out the best in root vegetables – they become tender and sweet, lending a welcome richness to any winter meal. Don't worry if you haven't got all the vegetables on the list below, you can substitute any root vegetables you like: swedes, turnips, shallots and red onions are all enhanced by roasting.

Roasted Root Vegetables are wonderfully versatile: enjoy them as a side dish or chill them and enjoy (at room temperature) as a salad, dressed with olive oil and lemon juice. They also make a wonderful vegetarian main: stir them into cooked pasta along with a splash of olive oil, then top with grated cheese. If you've got access to a liquidiser, you can turn Roasted Root Vegetables into a creamy soup by pureeing them and adding vegetable stock to thin.

2 large baking potatoes, peeled and cut into 3cm chunks

2 large carrots, chopped into 3cm chunks

1 small butternut squash, peeled and cut into 3cm chunks

2 parsnips, peeled and cut into 3cm chunks

1 large sweet potato, peeled and cut into 3cm chunks

50ml olive oil

2 teaspoons of dried rosemary, crushed

Salt and ground black pepper, to taste

Preheat the oven to 200 degrees C. Put the chunks of baking potato into a saucepan, cover with cold water and add a pinch of salt. Bring to the boil over high heat, cover and simmer for 10 minutes. While the potatoes are cooking, spread all of the other vegetables into a large baking dish in a single layer. After the potatoes have cooked for 10 minutes, drain them well and add them to the other vegetables in the baking dish.

Drizzle over the olive oil, sprinkle with the rosemary, salt and pepper, and mix well so all the vegetables are coated with oil and herbs. Roast, uncovered, for about 1 hour or until all the vegetables are soft and beginning to brown. Stir once or twice during the cooking time, if desired – the vegetables will brown more evenly if you do.

****

SAUCES AND DRESSINGS

Cucumber Raita
(Serves 4-6)

This cooling Indian sauce is often served with curries. The authentic version calls for fresh mint, but if that's not available, bottled mint sauce makes an acceptable substitute. Cucumber Raita is also good with kebabs or other grilled meat.

250ml yoghurt

½ teaspoon salt

½ teaspoon sugar

1/2 cucumber, peeled, seeded and finely chopped or grated

1 tablespoon chopped fresh mint or mint sauce (if desired)

Ground black pepper

Combine all ingredients and mix well. Chill for at least 30 minutes before using. Sprinkle with ground pepper just before serving.

Mock Rouille
(Serves 2-4, recipe can be doubled)

Mock Rouille is the cheat's version of the classic French sauce that is traditionally served with fish, soup and bouillabaisse. Mediterranean Fish Soup (page 8) and Provencal Vegetable Stew (page 78) both depend on it for flavour and a bit of a kick. If you've got any rouille left over, use it as a spread for prawn sandwiches or as a topping for plain grilled fish.

75ml mayonnaise

1 garlic clove, crushed but left whole so it can be easily removed

½ - 1 teaspoon chilli powder or ½ teaspoon hot pepper sauce (or to taste)

Mix all of the ingredients in a small bowl and refrigerate for at least 1 hour, to allow flavours to blend. When ready to serve, remove the garlic clove.

Tzatziki
(Serves 4)

Tzatziki is a close relative of the Indian raita, but the Greek version of this yoghurt-based sauce always includes garlic. Greek cooks sometimes add olive oil and lemon juice, too. Tzatziki is incredibly versatile – not only does it make a refreshing dip for raw vegetables or pitta bread, but it can also be used as an ingredient to turn a plain meal into something special. I've included a few recipe suggestions below.

250ml Greek yoghurt
½ cucumber, peeled, seeded and finely chopped or grated
½ teaspoon salt
1-2 cloves garlic, according to taste, very finely minced

Combine all ingredients and mix well. Chill for at least 30 minutes before using. If you'd like to vary the recipe, feel free to add chopped fresh mint (or a bit of mint sauce), fresh dill, fresh lemon juice and/or olive oil, to taste.

Tzatziki suggestions (to serve 2, all recipes can be doubled):

1. Roast two salmon fillets (defrosted) in a 200 degree C oven for no more than 20 minutes (check after 15 minutes). They will come out juicy and moist. Top with a couple of tablespoons of tzatziki and serve with Greek Rice Pilaf (page 133) and a green salad.
2. Cook 250g of pasta (a small shape such as elbows is best). Drain well. Blend 150ml tzatziki and a tin of

well-drained tuna or salmon (broken up with a fork) into the pasta. Add some cooked peas, if desired. Serve with plenty of fresh ground black pepper. This dish can also be served cold as a pasta salad.

3. Create a **Salade Nicoise**, using seasonal ingredients of your own choosing. Arrange any (or all) of the following ingredients on a bed of salad leaves: cooked prawns, grilled tuna steaks (or a tin of tuna), good quality anchovies, steamed green beans, diced boiled potatoes, tomato quarters, sliced cucumber, Greek olives, sliced red onion, etc., etc. Top with generous dollops of tzatziki rather than the traditional French dressing.

4. Tzatziki makes a fantastic salad dressing, and it is also quite low in fat when compared to traditional vinaigrettes.

5. Cut 400g of defrosted Lundy lamb (or chicken breast) into large cubes. Combine 100ml olive oil, 30ml lemon juice, 1 teaspoon dried oregano, a large pinch of salt and ground black pepper to taste in a non-metallic bowl. Add the meat to the marinade, mix well, cover and chill for at least 1 hour (overnight is fine). Grill the meat, turning often, until cooked. Serve with boiled rice, topped with tzatziki.

Honey Mustard Vinaigrette
(Makes about 500ml)

This creamy dressing is very versatile. Mix Honey Mustard Vinaigrette with a beetroot and apple salad (add a few nuts for extra crunch) or stir it into grated carrots for a cooling complement to a curry. It is also good as a dip for raw vegetables or as a sauce for grilled fish or chicken or steamed vegetables.

75ml vinegar

75ml Dijon mustard

75ml honey

250ml olive or vegetable oil

Salt and pepper to taste

Whisk together the vinegar and mustard in a small bowl. Continue to whisk whilst drizzling in the honey, then the oil. Mix until well blended and season to taste. Store in the fridge until needed.

BAKING

Lundy kitchens don't have scales, so quantities in the Baking chapter have been specified in metric volumes rather than weights. To make the recipes in this chapter, you will need to measure your ingredients using the Pyrex jug found in every Lundy kitchen. Precision is important in baking so when measuring dry ingredients in the jug, be sure to level their tops to ensure accuracy. You will soon find that baking 'Lundy style' is as easy as baking at home!

****

Chocolate Mayonnaise Cake
(Serves 8)

How many times have you planned to bake a cake, only to discover that you don't have enough butter or eggs? Well, mayonnaise makes a brilliant substitute. This scrummy chocolate cake will surprise your family and friends – don't tell them what the secret ingredient is until after they've tasted it!

500ml self-raising flour

125ml cocoa

pinch salt

250ml demerara sugar

180ml mayonnaise (full fat)

250ml water

Raspberry jam and whipped cream, to finish

Icing sugar

Preheat the oven to 180 degrees C. Grease the bottoms and sides of two sandwich tins (19-20cm) then dust them with cocoa (or plain flour), shaking out the excess. In a medium bowl, mix together the flour, cocoa and salt. In a large bowl, whisk the sugar, mayonnaise and water until well mixed.

Add the dry ingredients to the liquid mixture and stir until well blended. Divide the batter evenly between the prepared sandwich tins and smooth the tops. Bake for 25 minutes or until the cakes test done. Remove them from the oven and run a knife around the edges of the tins to release the cakes. Allow the cakes to cool completely in the tins and then remove. Sandwich the cakes together with raspberry jam and whipped cream in between the layers, and dust the top with icing sugar.

****

Victoria Sponge
(Serves 8)

A teatime classic – who can resist it? If you haven't got raspberry jam, strawberry makes a fine substitute.

225g butter, softened
250ml caster sugar
4 large eggs, lightly beaten
350ml self-raising flour
Raspberry jam
Whipped cream (if desired)
Icing sugar, for dusting

Preheat the oven to 180 degrees C. Grease two sandwich tins (19-20cm) and dust them with flour, shaking out the excess. Cream together the butter and sugar, beating until light and fluffy. Keep beating until the mixture is a very pale colour. Add the eggs to the sugar and butter mixture a little at a time, beating until they are thoroughly mixed in.

Add the flour gradually, stirring gently until the mixture is completely blended. Divide it evenly between the two sandwich tins, smooth the tops and bake for 20-25 minutes, until risen and golden in colour and the cakes test done. Remove the tins from the oven, run a knife around the edges of the cakes to release them, then cool on a rack (in the tins) for 10 minutes.

Remove the cakes from tins and return to the rack to finish cooling. When completely cool, sandwich the cakes together with raspberry jam and whipped cream (if using), and dust the top generously with icing sugar.

****

Scones
(Makes 12-15 scones)

Everyone wants to know the secret to light and fluffy scones, but it is really quite simple: do not overwork the dough. The lighter your touch, the lighter your scones will be. This basic scone recipe calls for self-raising flour, but if you haven't got any, you can substitute 400ml of plain flour plus 2 teaspoons of baking powder.

400ml self-raising flour
2 tablespoons caster sugar
75g butter
1 egg, beaten
90ml milk

Preheat the oven to 200 degrees C. In a large bowl, rub the butter into the flour until the mixture looks like flaky breadcrumbs. Add the sugar. Add the beaten egg to the mixture, then gradually add the milk. Add just enough milk to create a soft dough. Turn the dough out onto a floured work surface. Pat it gently into a circle about 2.5cm thick and then gently roll it out (only one or two rolls) with a rolling pin.

Cut out scones using the floured rim of a small glass (5-6cm diameter), cutting down in one motion and lifting the glass off without twisting it. Gently pat together the remaining dough, roll it out again and continue to cut out scones until the dough is gone.

To bake, place the scones in sandwich tins so their edges are just touching. (If you are planning to eat the scones later that day, you can cover the tins for a couple of hours with a clean tea towel until ready to bake.) Brush the tops lightly with milk and bake for 12-15 minutes or until risen and fully cooked. Cool the scones slightly and then pull them apart. Serve the scones with butter, jam and/or clotted cream.

****

Fruit and Nut Cookies
(Makes about 25 cookies)

These chewy, moreish biscuits are filled with good-for-you ingredients. They make a fun rainy day project for children, who love rolling the dough into balls. If you've got muesli to use up, you can substitute 700ml muesli for the oats, raisins and nuts.

400ml porridge oats

150ml raisins or other dried fruit, chopped if large

150ml nuts, chopped

200ml self-raising flour

150ml soft brown sugar

3 tablespoons honey

1 egg, beaten

100g butter (or margarine), melted and cooled slightly

Preheat the oven to 180 degrees C and grease a baking tray well. Combine the oats, raisins, nuts, flour and sugar in a large bowl. Stir the honey, egg and butter together, add to the dry ingredients and mix well.

Roll dough into 3cm balls and place them on the baking tray, leaving 3cm space between them. Bake for 12-15 minutes, or until lightly golden. Allow the cookies to cool for 5 minutes, then remove them from the baking trays to cool completely on a wire rack. When cool, store the cookies in an airtight tin.

Fiona's Shortbread

This is one of the easiest recipes I know, but also one of the best. It was given to me by my dear friend, Fiona McKenzie. Don't be fooled by its simplicity – these homemade shortbread biscuits rival the finest brands.

100g butter
350ml plain flour
100ml sugar
Additional sugar, for sprinkling

Preheat the oven to 170 degrees C. In a medium sized saucepan, melt the butter over low heat. Stir in the flour and sugar until well blended.

Transfer the mixture to a sandwich tin and pat it down firmly so it is smooth and evenly distributed. Prick the shortbread all over with a fork and bake it for 15-20 minutes, or until light golden brown and firm.

Remove the shortbread from the oven, sprinkle it with sugar and cut it into pieces while still hot. Cool the shortbread in the tin. When completely cool, remove it from the tin and store in an airtight container.

Variation: sprinkle 60g chopped chocolate over the shortbread before baking (press it lightly into the surface).

DESSERTS

Apple and Banana Crumble
(Serves 6-8)

This variation on the traditional crumble includes bananas, which add a lovely caramelised flavour. Oats and chopped nuts add a bit of crunch to the topping. If you don't have porridge oats, feel free to substitute muesli (250ml) for the oats and chopped nuts. You can use almost any fruit in a crumble - try pears, plums, summer berries or peaches, depending on what's in season.

Filling:

4 tablespoons soft light brown sugar

5 medium-large apples, peeled, cored, and cut into 2.5cm chunks

3-4 ripe bananas, peeled and cut into chunks

Crumble Topping:

170ml plain flour

170ml soft light brown sugar

1/2 teaspoon ground cinnamon

170ml porridge oats

80ml chopped nuts

110g butter, cut into pieces

Preheat the oven to 180 degrees C. Grease a large ovenproof dish. In a large bowl combine the sugar and fruit and mix well. Transfer to the prepared dish.

Make the Crumble Topping: Combine the flour, sugar, ground cinnamon, salt, oats and nuts in a large bowl. Cut the butter into small pieces and rub into the flour mixture until the crumbs are about the size of peas. Spread the Crumble Topping evenly over the fruit.

Bake for approximately 45-50 minutes or until the fruit is bubbling and the topping is golden brown and crisp. If the crumble browns too quickly, lay a sheet of aluminium foil loosely over the top. Remove the crumble from the oven and cool it for a few minutes before serving. Serve warm with cream or vanilla ice cream. Cool and chill leftovers and reheat before serving.

****

Rich Chocolate Sauce
(Serves 4-6)

This dessert sauce is a real treat for chocolate lovers. It is served warm and is fantastic spooned over your favourite flavour of ice cream or a berry sorbet. Rich Chocolate Sauce is also extremely versatile – see the additional dessert ideas below.

250ml double cream

200g good quality chocolate (70% is best), finely chopped

Bring the cream to the boil in a medium saucepan, then pour the hot cream over the chocolate in a bowl. Whisk well until the chocolate is melted. Keep the sauce warm until ready to use. If you have any leftover sauce, cover it and keep it in the fridge. Reheat very gently (don't boil) before using.

Here are a few recipe ideas using Rich Chocolate Sauce, but feel free to use your imagination!

1. **Old-fashioned Banana Splits:** for each person, slice a banana lengthways and then cut each length in half. Arrange the banana quarters in a dish and top with a large scoop of vanilla ice cream. Drizzle with warm Chocolate Sauce and sprinkle with chopped nuts.
2. **Pears with Chocolate Sauce:** poach pears in a sugar syrup with a dash of cinnamon. Serve warm, drizzled with warm Chocolate Sauce.

3. **Chocolate-dipped strawberries:** for each person, prepare a serving of fresh strawberries. Serve with an individual dish of warm Chocolate Sauce for dipping.

4. **Chocolate Filling/Icing:** use Rich Chocolate Sauce to fill and/or ice a plain cake, or just drizzle over the top of the cake before serving.

****

English Soup (Zuppa Inglese)
(Serves 6)

Soup for pudding? That sounds odd! But English Soup isn't a soup at all – in fact, it is an Italian version of our traditional English trifle. Zuppa Inglese is an excellent way to use up leftover bits of cake, chocolate, fruit and nuts and it is a simple dessert to prepare. But be sure to make it early in the day, because Zuppa Inglese must be chilled for at least two hours before it can be served.

75g sachet Bird's custard, prepared according to packet directions

1 small loaf cake (Madeira, fruit or ginger), cut into cubes

50ml sloe gin (or any other sweet liqueur)

500ml fresh fruit: peaches, plums or pears (chopped), strawberries (sliced) or any other berries

60g plain chocolate, chopped

Handful of nuts, chopped

Prepare the custard and set aside. Place half of the cake cubes in the bottom of a large bowl (or individual serving dishes) and sprinkle with 1/3 of the sloe gin or other liqueur. Spoon over 1/3 of the custard and top with half of the fruit and chopped chocolate.

Cover with the remaining cake, drizzle with another 1/3 of the liqueur and spoon over the second 1/3 of the custard. Top with the remaining fruit and chocolate and sprinkle with the rest of the liqueur. Finish the layering with the remaining 1/3 of the custard topped with the chopped nuts. Cover the pudding with cling film and chill for 2-3 hours (or up to 24 hours) before serving cold.

****

Ginger Baked Pears
(Serves 6)

A rich and warming winter dessert, as well as a good way to use up some leftover biscuits. If you haven't got any ginger nuts, digestives or shortbread will do very well. An easy way to crush the biscuits is to put them into a plastic bag, close it tightly, and bash it with a rolling pin. If you put Ginger Baked Pears into the oven before you sit down to dinner, they will be ready just in time for dessert.

6 ripe pears, halved lengthways and cored
12 ginger nut biscuits, crushed
6 large pieces of crystallised ginger, finely chopped
110g butter, melted (plus extra for greasing)
1 large egg yolk
80ml runny honey
Double cream or vanilla ice cream, to serve

Preheat the oven to 200 degrees C. and grease a baking dish large enough to hold all the pear halves (you will want them to fit tightly in the dish, so that they stay upright). In a bowl, mix the crushed biscuits, ginger, melted butter and egg yolk together. Place the pears in the prepared dish and stuff them with the filling, mounding it in the centre and spreading it out to the edges. Drizzle with the honey and bake for 30-40 minutes, until the pears are soft and the topping slightly browned. Serve two halves per person, with cream or ice cream.

Fruity Bread Pudding
(Serves 4-6)

The fruit gives this old-fashioned favourite a healthy new twist. Put Fruity Bread Pudding into the oven before you sit down to eat. It will be ready in 45 minutes and is at its best when served warm with pouring custard.

8 slices of bread, buttered

500ml fresh or frozen fruit (berries, thinly sliced peaches or nectarines, etc.)

1 teaspoon grated lemon peel

3 eggs

150ml sugar

700ml single cream or whole milk

Heat the oven to 180 degrees. Arrange the buttered bread (so it overlaps) in an ovenproof dish. Spread the fruit over the top and sprinkle with the lemon peel.

In a bowl, beat together the eggs and sugar, then add the cream or milk and mix well. Pour the egg mixture over the bread and fruit and cook for 45 minutes (or until a knife inserted in the centre comes out clean). Serve warm with pouring custard.

Lundy Mess
(Serves 4)

Based on the famous Eton Mess, this quick, no-cook dessert will please children and adults alike. An easy way to crush the biscuits is to put them into a plastic bag, close it tightly, and bash it with a rolling pin. Make Lundy Mess just before you plan to eat it, so that the biscuits stay crunchy.

400ml double cream

4 tablespoons honey

120g Hobnobs or similar biscuits, crushed

120g frozen raspberries, defrosted and crushed

Using a whisk, whip the cream and honey together until the cream has thickened and stands in soft peaks. Add the crushed biscuits and raspberries and stir to create a marbled effect. Spoon into glasses or bowls and serve immediately.

Chocolate Honey Mousse
(Serves 4)

Chocolate Honey Mousse is rich and decadent, the sort of pudding you'd expect to find in a fine restaurant. Yet with only four ingredients, this elegant dessert is quick and easy to prepare. It's lovely as is but if you feel like gilding the lily, you can garnish the finished mousse with additional whipped cream and top with berries or a few chopped nuts.

300ml double cream, chilled

175g plain chocolate, chopped

2 tablespoons honey

2 teaspoons milk

Additional double cream for topping (if desired)

Berries or chopped nuts (if desired)

In a medium pan over low heat, stir 100ml of the cream, the chocolate and the honey until smooth. Set it aside to cool, stirring occasionally.

In a large bowl, stir the remaining 200ml cream together with the milk. Whip the mixture until soft peaks form (do not over beat). Fold the whipped cream into the cooled chocolate mixture, in two additions. Divide the mousse amongst 8 ramekins or cups and chill until set, about 2 hours. Serve topped with additional whipped cream and/or berries or chopped nuts, if desired. This mousse is best served on the day it is made.

DRINKS

Easy Lemon Cordial
(Makes about 500ml)

An old-fashioned, refreshing summer drink, Easy Lemon Cordial keeps well in the fridge.

250ml sugar

125ml water

3 lemons (cut the rind from 1 of the lemons into thin strips)

Pinch of salt

Boil the sugar, water, lemon rind and salt for 5 minutes, then remove the mixture from the heat. While it is cooling, juice all 3 lemons. After the sugar mixture has cooled, add the lemon juice and stir well. Pour the cordial through a sieve into a jar, cover and store in the fridge.

To serve, mix 2 tablespoons of lemon cordial with 1 glass of water (still or sparkling). Or add 1 tablespoon cordial plus 2 tablespoons of orange or pineapple juice to a glass of water.

Mulled Wine
(Serves 6)

A glass of Mulled Wine is the perfect way to warm up a cold winter's night. Do not allow the wine to boil, or the alcohol will evaporate!

750ml red wine

½ teaspoon ground cinnamon

60ml honey

1 bay leaf (optional)

Juice of 1 orange

Juice of ½ lemon

2 cm wide strip of orange zest

Combine all the ingredients in a saucepan and heat over medium-low heat until the mixture just begins to simmer. Simmer very gently for 15-20 minutes to blend the flavours. Do not allow the wine to boil. Remove the bay leaf and orange zest before serving. Serve hot.

SALMAGUNDI

This chapter salutes the spirit of the Salmagundi, a 17th century English salad dish. Take some cooked meats, seafood and vegetables and combine them with fruit, leaves, nuts and flowers. Dress the entire concoction with oil, vinegar and rare spices, and you've got a Salmagundi – an exotic dish, fit for a king.

Our 21st century Salmagundi takes an equally inventive approach towards ingredients. If you've got a bit of mayonnaise you'd like to use up, take a look at Salmagundi. You'll find it here (along with many other ingredients), all listed alphabetically. To inspire you, each ingredient is linked to recipes and suggestions for easy dishes. Give Salmagundi a try – you will soon be turning those odd bits of food into tasty meals. And at the same time, you will be helping to keep Lundy green, by minimising food waste.

APPLES:

Recipes:

Apple and Blue Cheese Salad (page 20)

Pork with Apples and Ginger (page 34)

Spicy Grilled Mackerel with Beetroot Salsa (page 61)

Apple and Banana Crumble (page 108)

Suggestions:

- Make **Apple Sauce**: peel apples and chop into chunks. Place in a saucepan with enough water to cover the bottom of the pan and add sugar to taste. Bring to the boil and cook gently, stirring occasionally, until apples have melted down. Add a bit of ground cinnamon, if desired.
- Melt a knob of butter in a frying pan, add thin slices of peeled apple and a dash of cinnamon, if desired. Cook gently until apple is soft and serve with a pork roast.

BACON:

Recipes:

Potato, Leek and Bacon Soup (page 16)

Stuffed Chicken Breasts (page 52)

Potato Gratin with Cheese and Ham (page 90)

Suggestions:

- Make **Bacon and Avocado Sandwiches**: cook streaky bacon and drain thoroughly. Slice a ripe avocado and lay it on a slice of wholemeal toast that has been spread lightly with mayonnaise. Top with bacon and another slice of toast. Delicious!
- Make a **Bacon and Beetroot Salad (page 130)**

BISCUITS:

Recipes:

Ginger Baked Pears (page 114)

Lundy Mess (page 116)

Suggestions:

- Make **Ice Cream Sandwiches**: soften ice cream (any flavour you like). Sandwich softened ice cream between two biscuits, wrap and re-freeze.
- Make **Grilled Peaches with Biscuit Topping**: Peel 2 ripe peaches (or nectarines), remove stones and slice into 1cm thick slices. Mix them with 2 teaspoons of lemon juice and 1 tablespoon soft brown sugar. Arrange in a single layer in a buttered oven dish and grill for 5-7 minutes, or until they are tender. In a small bowl, combine 1 teaspoon soft brown sugar, 2 crumbled biscuits (shortbread or ginger) and 1 tablespoon butter, cut into bits. Spread biscuit mixture over peaches and grill for 2 minutes or until topping is golden. Serve warm with cream or ice cream (serves 2, recipe can be doubled).

BLUE CHEESE:

Recipes:

Apple and Blue Cheese Salad (page 20)

Blue Cheese Burgers (page 35)

Easy Pizza (page 72)

Potato Gratin with Cheese and Ham (page 90)

Suggestions:

- Make **Blue Cheese Dressing**: in a small bowl mix equal quantities of mayonnaise and soured cream (or yoghurt). Add crumbled blue cheese, and a little vinegar or lemon juice and mix well. Use as a dip for raw vegetables or thin with a little milk to use as a dressing for a plain green salad.

BREAD:

Recipes:

Soutzsoukakia (page 24)

Fruity Bread Pudding (page 115)

Suggestions:

- Make **Croutons**: cut the crusts off 3 slices of bread and cut the bread into 1cm cubes. Melt 25g butter in a frying pan, add 1 clove garlic (if desired) and the bread cubes. Fry over low heat, turning the bread frequently until the cubes are golden brown on all sides. Remove from the heat and use the croutons in soups, salads or as a garnish.
- Make **French Toast**: Whisk 3 eggs with 120ml milk, 1 teaspoon of sugar and a pinch of cinnamon (if desired). Dip 4 slices of bread into the egg mixture, allowing the egg to soak into the bread. Melt a knob of butter in a frying pan and fry the bread on both sides until golden (about 2 minutes per side). Serve topped with fruit (berries, sliced peaches, poached apples or pears, etc.) and drizzled with honey.

French toast is also good topped with melted jam: in a saucepan mix jam with a bit of water. Cook, stirring, over low heat until warmed through.

BROCCOLI:

Recipes:

Oriental Salmon (page 56)

Pasta al Pesto (page 70)

Stir Fried Vegetables (page 87)

Suggestions:

- Steam broccoli florets, then refresh them under cold water and add to salads
- Cut into florets and serve raw with a dip, e.g., **Honey Mustard Vinaigrette (page 98), Blue Cheese Dressing (page 122)** or **Curry Dip (page 132)**
- Fill an omelette with leftover cooked broccoli and grated cheddar cheese

BUTTER:

Recipes:

Fish Chowder (page 12)

Salmon with Red Wine Sauce (page 62)

Pasta with Blue Cheese and Spinach (page 67)

Most of the recipes in the Baking chapter (page 99)

Apple and Banana Crumble (page 108)

Ginger Baked Pears (page 114)

Suggestions:

- Make **Honey Butter**: blend 4 parts softened butter with 1 part honey. Add a pinch of ground cinnamon, if desired. Store in the fridge. Honey Butter is delicious on toast or muffins or melted over pancakes.

CARROTS:

Recipes:

Irish Lamb Soup (page 10)

Soupe au Pistou (page 14)

Chinese-style Cabbage Salad (page 21)

Moroccan Lamb Stew (page 26)

Chicken Cacciatore (page 50)

Roasted Root Vegetables (page 92)

Suggestions:

- Shred carrots, dress with **French Vinaigrette (page 127)** and serve as part of a composed salad.
- Make a **Carrot and Raisin Salad**: shred enough carrots to serve your family. Add raisins (1 part raisins to 4 parts carrots). Mix carrots and raisins with enough mayonnaise to moisten and add a bit of grated onion for additional flavour (if desired). Chill for at least 30 minutes before serving.
- Make **Carrot and Sweet Potato Mash**: boil peeled, cubed sweet potatoes with carrot chunks until tender. Add butter, milk, salt and pepper to taste and mash well.

CELERY:

Recipes:

Mediterranean Fish Soup (page 8)

Apple and Blue Cheese Salad (page 20)

Jambalaya (page 44)

Chicken Cacciatore (page 50)

Suggestions:

- Make **Braised Celery in Cheese Sauce**: chop celery into 3cm lengths. Heat butter in a large pan and sauté some chopped onion, then add the celery and a

few tablespoons of water and cook (covered) until tender. While the celery is cooking, prepare a white sauce using butter, flour and milk. Stir some grated cheese (cheddar or blue) into the sauce and mix the cheese sauce with the celery. Serve over cooked pasta or rice as a vegetarian main.
- Stuff celery sticks with peanut butter for a healthy treat.

CHEDDAR CHEESE:

Recipes:

Chilli con Carne (page 38)

Pasta al Pesto (page 70)

Easy Pizza (page 72)

Hasselback Potatoes (page 89)

Potato Gratin with Cheese and Ham (page 90)

Suggestions:
- Make **Tuna Melts**: mix a tin of drained and flaked tuna with mayonnaise and spread the mixture on toast. Top with grated cheddar and grill until cheese melts.

CHORIZO:

Recipes:

Spanish Chicken Stew (page 40)

Jambalaya (page 44)

Easy Pizza (page 72)

Suggestions:
- Make a quick **Bean and Chorizo Soup**: Put a tin of chopped tomatoes and one tin of water into a saucepan. Chop some chorizo and add it to the pan along with a tin of drained beans and a crumbled stock cube. Shred a wedge of cabbage or some

spinach, add to the pan and cook, covered, for 5-7 minutes or until the vegetables are soft.

CHUTNEY:

Recipes:

Country Captain (page 48)

Vegetable Biryani (page 84)

Suggestions:

- Make a **Curry Dip (page 132)**
- Mix a spoonful into **Stir Fried Vegetables (page 87)** and cook along with the vegetables. It will give the dish a bit of spicy sweetness.
- Blend a tablespoon of chutney into a plain vinaigrette dressing. This dressing is especially good with a beetroot and apple salad or spooned over a pear and blue cheese salad.

COURGETTES:

Recipes:

Soupe au Pistou (page 14)

Provencal Vegetable Stew (page 78)

Stir Fried Vegetables (page 87)

Ratatouille (page 88)

Suggestions:

- Grate raw courgettes and serve as part of a composed salad
- Make **Creamed Courgettes**: grate enough courgettes to serve your guests. Melt some butter in a large pan and add the courgettes. Cook over low heat, stirring occasionally, until the courgettes have softened and all the liquid has evaporated. Remove from the heat and stir in enough double cream or Greek yoghurt to moisten the courgettes. Season to taste and serve.

CUCUMBER:

Recipes:

Marinated Cucumbers (page 23)

Summer Pasta (page 68)

Cold Noodles with Spicy Peanut Sauce (page 74)

Cucumber Raita (page 94)

Tzatziki (page 96)

Suggestions:

- Make an **Oriental-style Salad**: combine a tin of bean sprouts (drained) with thinly sliced cucumber and some shredded carrot. Make a dressing with 60ml vegetable oil, 2 tablespoons vinegar, 1 tablespoon soy sauce and 1 teaspoon sugar. Mix dressing thoroughly with vegetables and chill for at least 30 minutes before serving. Sprinkle with chopped peanuts, if desired.
- Cucumber can be cooked as part of a **Vegetable Stir Fry (page 87).** Peel and remove the seeds, then slice on the diagonal. Add to the pan with your other vegetables and cook briefly, until just tender.

DIJON MUSTARD:

Recipes:

Blue Cheese Burgers (page 35)

Chicken with Mustard Sauce (page 42)

Roast Salmon with Garlic and Mustard (page 55)

Honey Mustard Vinaigrette (page 98)

Suggestions:

- Make a traditional **French Vinaigrette**: whisk 1 tablespoon of Dijon mustard with 1 tablespoon of red wine vinegar. While continuing to whisk constantly, adding 240ml olive oil, very slowly, until the mixture emulsifies. Add salt and ground black pepper to taste. Store in a jar in the fridge until needed. If mixture thickens too much, whisk in a little water.

- Make **Honey Mustard Chicken**: blend 3 tablespoons of Dijon mustard with 1 tablespoon runny honey. Spread over chicken portions before roasting in a hot oven.
- A dollop of Dijon mustard enhances a cheese sauce and is particularly good with cauliflower cheese.

DRIED FRUITS:

Recipes:

Moroccan Lamb Stew (page 26)

Country Captain (page 48)

Spinach and Chick Pea Stew (page 75)

Fruit and Nut Cookies (page 106)

Suggestions:

- Make a **Carrot and Raisin Salad (page 124)**
- Make **Stewed Fruits**: combine dried fruits in a saucepan with large chunks of peeled apple or pear. Pour over red wine (or fruit juice) to cover. Add cinnamon to taste. Simmer gently until fruits are soft. Stewed Fruits are lovely topped with yoghurt or cream for dessert, or (if made with fruit juice) mixed with porridge for breakfast.
- Make a **Middle Eastern Rice Pilaf**: melt butter in a saucepan and sauté some finely minced onion. Add rice and stir until the grains have gone white – do not let it burn. Add enough water and stock cubes (chicken or vegetable) to suit the amount of rice, then stir in some chopped dried apricots, raisins or sultanas. Bring to the boil, cover and simmer until all the liquid is absorbed. Stir and serve with lamb or a vegetable stew.

EGGS:

Recipes:

Vegetable Biryani (page 84)

Victoria Sponge (page 102)

Scones (page 104)

Fruit and Nut Cookies (page 106)

Ginger Baked Pears (page 114)

Suggestions:

- Make **Devilled Eggs**: hard boil eggs, cut them in half lengthways and scoop out the yolks. Mash the yolks together with mayonnaise, a bit of Dijon mustard and some grated onion and/or hot pepper sauce. Spoon the yolk mixture back into the egg halves and chill till ready to serve. Perfect for picnics!
- Make **Potato Salad**: Peel and chop potatoes into bite-sized chunks. Cook them in boiling water until tender, drain and cool. Mix with chopped hard-boiled egg, chopped celery and some chopped red onion. Add mayonnaise, salt and pepper and a bit of mustard (to taste), and mix well. Chill until ready to serve.

FETA CHEESE:

Recipes:

Greek Pasta Salad (page 18)

Lamb with Lentils and Rosemary (page 30)

Stuffed Chicken Breasts (page 52)

Prawns with Feta (page 64)

Summer Pasta (page 68)

Suggestions:

- Make a **Chick Pea Salad**: Mix a tin of drained chick peas with some chopped tomatoes and chopped red

onion (or spring onion). Make a dressing with olive oil, lemon juice and salt and pepper to taste, and mix it with the beans. Sprinkle the salad with crumbled feta cheese before serving.
- Top defrosted white fish fillets with chopped tomato, minced garlic and a bit of dried oregano. Sprinkle with crumbled feta and roast in a hot oven for 10-15 minutes.

HONEY:

Recipes:

Honey Mustard Vinaigrette (page 98)

Fruit and Nut Cookies (page 106)

Ginger Baked Pears (page 114)

Lundy Mess (page 116)

Chocolate Honey Mousse (page 117)

Mulled Wine (page 119)

Suggestions:

- Make **Honey Butter (page 123)**
- Make **Scottish Cranachan (page 136)**
- Make **Teriyaki Marinade** for beef, chicken or fish **(page 138)**

HORSERADISH SAUCE:

Recipes:

Beef Braised in Ale (page 36)

Mackerel with Horseradish Cream Lentils (page 58)

Suggestions:

- Make a **Bacon & Beetroot Salad**: Cut 4 medium cooked beetroot into cubes and add 4 spring onions, thinly sliced. Cut 2 cooked bacon rashers into cubes and add them to the vegetables. In a separate bowl,

stir together 100ml Greek yoghurt, 1 tablespoon lemon juice and 1-2 tablespoons horseradish sauce (to taste). Add the yoghurt mixture to the beetroot, onions and bacon and mix well. Chill the salad until ready to serve. This salad goes well with cold roast beef, or it can be served on toasted bread as a Scandinavian-style open sandwich.
- Make a **Russian Mayonnaise (page 132)**
- Make a fresh **Tartare Sauce**: combine 125ml mayonnaise with 1 tablespoon chopped capers, 1 rounded teaspoon horseradish sauce, 1 rounded teaspoon mustard and 1 finely chopped spring onion. Serve with grilled or fried fish or with fishcakes.
- Make **Horseradish Mash**: simply add 1-2 tablespoons of horseradish sauce to mashed potatoes. Excellent with roast beef or salmon.

HUMMUS:

Suggestions:
- Top defrosted salmon fillets with a mixture of hummus, finely minced garlic and crumbled feta cheese before roasting in a hot oven for 15-20 minutes.
- Make a salad dressing by thinning hummus with lemon juice (e.g., 1/2 tub hummus with the juice of half a lemon). If desired, add a tablespoon of olive oil and mix well. Good with any salad, but especially with grated carrots.
- Make a **Pesto Party Dip (page 135)**

LEMONS:

Recipes:

Greek Pasta Salad (page 18)

Moroccan Lamb Stew (page 26)

Greek Chicken with Oregano (page 54)

Easy Lemon Cordial (page 118)

Suggestions:

- Before roasting a chicken, place half a lemon in the cavity, along with some herbs of your choice. The lemon will help to keep the bird moist and will also impart a lovely flavour.
- Make **Vegetables in Lemon Butter**: Melt 50g butter in a large pan and add enough vegetables to serve 4 people (green beans, sliced carrots and broccoli are all good). Add the juice of one lemon and salt to taste. Cook, uncovered, until the vegetables are crisp-tender, about 5-7 minutes.

MAYONNAISE:

Recipes:

Stuffed Chicken Breasts (page 52)

Cod with Parma Ham & Spicy Sauce (page 63)

Mock Rouille (page 95)

Chocolate Mayonnaise Cake (page 100)

Suggestions:

- Make **Tuna Melts:** mix a tin of drained and flaked tuna with mayonnaise and spread the mixture on toast. Top with grated cheddar and grill until cheese melts.
- Make a **Curry Dip**: mix one part mayonnaise with one part yoghurt. Add curry powder to taste, a bit of grated ginger, a squeeze of lemon juice and a tablespoon of chutney (chopped). Chill for at least 30 minutes and use as a dip for prawns or fresh vegetables.
- Make a **Russian Mayonnaise**: blend mayonnaise with ketchup, a dash of Worcestershire sauce and horseradish sauce to taste. Serve with prawns or poached salmon or as a garnish for hard-boiled eggs.
- Make a fresh **Tartare Sauce (page 131)**

MINT SAUCE:

Recipes:

Soutzsoukakia (page 24)

Cucumber Raita (page 94)

Tzatziki (page 96)

Suggestions:

- Stir a teaspoonful of mint sauce into cooked peas or boiled new potatoes to add a fresh flavour.
- Add a little mint sauce to a **Rice Salad (page 137)**
- Make a **Greek Rice Pilaf**: heat 2 tablespoons of oil in a large frying pan and add a large onion (chopped) and 2 garlic cloves (finely chopped). Cook until onion and garlic have softened. Mix in 500ml cooked rice, a couple of handfuls of fresh spinach (chopped) and 3 tablespoons of mint sauce. Cover and cook for 3-4 minutes, stirring occasionally. When the spinach is limp, remove from heat. Top with crumbled feta and serve immediately.

OLIVE OIL:

Recipes: many of the recipes in Lundy Cookery call for small amounts of olive oil, but here are some that use 50ml or more:

Greek Pasta Salad (page 18)

Beetroot and Orange Salad (page 22)

Summer Pasta (page 68)

Roasted Root Vegetables (page 92)

Honey Mustard Vinaigrette (page 98)

Suggestions:

- Make a traditional **French Vinaigrette (page 127)**
- Use in **Teriyaki Marinade (page 138)**

OLIVES:

Recipes:

Greek Pasta Salad (page 18)

Spanish Chicken Stew (page 40)

Prawns with Feta (page 64)

Easy Pizza (page 72)

Suggestions:

- Make a **Quick Pasta Sauce**: heat some olive oil in a saucepan with some chopped garlic. Add a tin of chopped tomatoes, some chopped olives, a few capers (if you've got them) and a tin of tuna (drained and flaked). Serve over cooked spaghetti.
- Make **Sicilian Broccoli**: heat olive oil in a frying pan and sauté some chopped garlic. Add broccoli (cut into bite sized pieces), 60ml water and half a stock cube. Cover and simmer until tender. Just before serving, stir in some chopped olives.

PEANUT BUTTER:

Recipes:

Middle Eastern Cauliflower Salad (page 17)

Cold Noodles with Spicy Peanut Sauce (page 74)

Suggestions:

- Make an Indonesian **Satay Sauce**: heat 1 tablespoon oil in a saucepan and cook 1 small onion (finely chopped) and 1 clove garlic (chopped) until lightly browned. Add 250ml water, 8 tablespoons peanut butter, 2 tablespoons soy sauce and 2 tablespoons sugar; cook and stir until well blended. Remove from heat and add 1 tablespoon lemon juice. Serve as a dipping sauce with grilled chicken or vegetables or mix into a stir fry and serve over rice.
- Make a **Peanut Butter & Yoghurt Spread**: Combine two parts yoghurt with one part peanut butter; add a

handful of raisins and a drizzle of honey, to taste. Mix everything together well and leave in the fridge overnight, to firm up. This spread is delicious on toast or crackers and can also be used as a filling or icing for a plain cake.
- Stuff peanut butter into celery sticks for a healthy treat

PESTO:

Recipes:

Soupe au Pistou (page 14)

Pasta al Pesto (page 70)

Risotto with Green Beans and Pesto (page 82)

Suggestions:

- Make **Pesto Mayonnaise**: blend 3 tablespoons mayonnaise with 2 tablespoons pesto. Mix with chopped cooked chicken for a delicious sandwich filling, or blend with cubed cooked potato and cold cooked green beans for a fantastic salad.
- Make **Pesto Mash**: stir a tablespoon of pesto into mashed potatoes to add an Italian touch to any meal.
- Make a **Pesto Bean Mash** by heating a tablespoon of olive oil and adding two drained tins of butter beans. Cook, stirring, for 3-4 minutes till heated through. Remove from heat, mash (leave some beans whole for a chunky texture) and stir in 2 tablespoons of pesto. Good with roast meats or served on toast.
- Stir a spoonful of pesto into any vegetable or bean soup (just before eating) to add lots of lovely flavour
- Make a **Pesto Party Dip**: blend a tub of ready-made hummus with 2 tablespoons of pesto. Top with crumbled feta cheese and serve with raw vegetables and/or warm pitta triangles. Delicious and so easy!

PORRIDGE OATS:

Recipes:

Fruit and Nut Cookies (page 106)

Apple and Banana Crumble (page 108)

Suggestions:

- Make a traditional **Scottish Cranachan** (serves 4): toast 150ml porridge oats in a dry frying pan until golden (watch carefully that they don't burn). Whip 250ml double cream until stiff, then fold in 2 tablespoons runny honey and 2 tablespoons malt whisky (if desired). Fold the toasted oatmeal into the whipped cream, then layer the cream mixture in glasses with 250g of raspberries (fresh or defrosted if frozen).
- Use porridge oats in place of coarse breadcrumbs in cooked dishes such as meatloaf.

POTATOES:

Recipes:

Many of the recipes in the Soups chapter (page 8)

Spanish Chicken Stew (page 40)

Pasta al Pesto (page 70)

Provencal Vegetable Stew (page 78)

Suggestions:

- Make a **Potato Tortilla**: Slice some potatoes and an onion very thinly and cook them in olive oil in a large pan until soft (about 20 minutes). Beat 4-6 eggs well in a bowl, add salt and pepper to taste, and pour over the potatoes. Cook over low heat for 10-12 minutes (or until set). Top with grated cheese and grill for 2 minutes or until cheese is melted.

RICE:

Recipes:

Jambalaya (page 44)

Vegetable Biryani (page 84)

Risotto with Green Beans and Pesto (page 82)

Suggestions:

- Add a handful of uncooked rice to any vegetable or bean soup and simmer gently for 15 -20 minutes. Leftover cooked rice should be added to soup just before serving – reheat just long enough to warm through.
- Make **Fried Rice**: heat some oil in a large pan, add chopped garlic and onions and cook until they soften. Add some chopped vegetables (broccoli, spring onions, carrots, peas, green beans and cabbage are all good) and stir fry until crisp-tender. Add leftover cooked rice, any cooked meat you might have in the fridge (chopped) and a splash of soy sauce. Continue to fry, stirring, until the mixture is piping hot.
- Make **Rice Salad**: Mix cooked rice with chopped vegetables (celery, red pepper, red onion and cooked peas all work well). Add vinaigrette dressing and mix thoroughly. Prawns or feta cheese also make good additions. Chill until ready to serve.
- Make a **Middle Eastern Rice Pilaf (page 128)** or a **Greek Rice Pilaf (page 133)**

SOY SAUCE:

Recipes:

Moroccan Lamb Stew (page 26)

Chicken Adobo (page 46)

Oriental Salmon (page 56)

Cold Noodles with Spicy Peanut Sauce (page 74)

Stir Fried Vegetables (page 87)

Suggestions:

- Make a **Teriyaki Marinade (page 138)**
- Make **Fried Rice (page 137)**
- Make a **Barbecue Sauce:** heat 2 tablespoons oil in a small saucepan; add 1 clove garlic (finely chopped) and 2 teaspoons finely chopped fresh ginger and stir fry for 3 minutes. Add 150ml ketchup, the juice of one lemon and 60ml soy sauce. Bring to the boil, stirring constantly. Reduce heat and simmer for 2 minutes, to blend the flavours. Remove from the heat. Use the sauce to baste chicken, pork or sausages, spooning over the meat during the last few minutes of cooking time. Or serve Barbecue Sauce over roasted cauliflower or carrots for a vegetarian feast.

VINEGAR:

Recipes:

Many of the recipes in the Salads chapter (page 17)

Orange-glazed Pork Chops (page 33)

Chicken Adobo (page 46)

Suggestions:

- Make a **Teriyaki Marinade** for beef, chicken or fish: mix 175ml vegetable oil, 60ml soy sauce, 1 finely minced clove garlic, 1 teaspoon grated fresh ginger, 3 tablespoons honey (or sugar) and 2 tablespoons vinegar in a small bowl. Place the meat in a non-reactive container (glass, plastic or stainless steel) and pour over the marinade. Refrigerate for 1-2 hours and then grill or barbecue.
- Make a quick **Burger Relish** by cooking 1 finely chopped onion and 1 tablespoon finely chopped ginger in 2 tablespoons olive oil until soft. Stir in 2 chopped tomatoes, 1 finely chopped peach (peeled and stone removed), 2 tablespoons brown sugar and

1 tablespoon each vinegar and water. Cook gently for 5 minutes, add a dash of hot pepper sauce (if desired) and cool before serving with beef or veggie burgers.

YOGHURT:

Recipes:

Middle Eastern Cauliflower Salad (page 17)

Vegetable Biryani (page 84)

Cucumber Raita (page 94)

Tzatziki (page 96)

Suggestions:

- Mix yoghurt with mayonnaise, soured cream or crème fraiche to lighten and extend the richer ingredient.
- **Yoghurt Parfaits** make a lovely dessert. Start with seasonal fresh fruit or defrosted frozen berries, jam (or honey) and biscuits. Crush biscuits. Melt jam in a saucepan over low heat with a little water, port, or any other liquid you fancy. Cut fruit into bite-sized pieces. Layer yoghurt, biscuits, fruit and melted jam (or honey) in a glass, ending with yoghurt as the top layer. Garnish with grated chocolate, if desired.
- Make a **Curry Dip (page 132)**
- Make **Peanut Butter & Yoghurt Spread (page 134)**

INDEX

About the Author

Ilene Sterns is an award-winning photographer and writer who visits Lundy as often as she can. Ilene's recipes have appeared in numerous publications including Mariner Newspapers and *Bon Appétit* magazine, and she recently won the 'Domestic Goddess' baking competition sponsored by Jordans Cereals. Ilene has attended courses at the Ashburton Cookery School and writes a regular cookery blog called 'All things EVERHOT'. She lives in the Cotswolds.